Strategies proven

Content instruction created just for the Upper SSAT. Practice to reinforce learning.

- ✓ Strategies to use for each section of the Upper Level SSAT
- ✓ Content instruction specific to the test and age-appropriate
- ✓ Drills and practice sets to build skills and confidence
- ✓ Full-length practice tests to show students what to expect and avoid surprises on test day (*Success on the Upper Level SSAT* and *The Best Unofficial Practice Tests* only)

Complete selection of Upper Level SSAT titles now available from Test Prep Works LLC:

Success on the Upper Level SSAT: A Complete Course
- Strategies for each section of the test
- Reading and vocabulary drills
- In-depth math content instruction with practice sets
- 1 full-length practice test

30 Days to Acing the Upper Level SSAT
- Strategies for each section of the test
- Fifteen "workouts", each providing practice problems and detailed explanations for every section of the test
- Perfect for additional practice or homework

The Best Unofficial Practice Tests for the Upper Level SSAT
- 2 additional full-length practice tests

Christa Abbott, M.Ed.

Are you an educator?

Incorporate materials from Test Prep Works into your test prep program

- Use the materials developed specifically for the test and level your students are taking

- Customize our books to fit your program

  - Choose content modules from any of our books – even from multiple books

  - Add your branding to the cover and title page

  - Greet your students with an introductory message

  - Create custom books with a one-time setup fee[1], then order copies at list price[2] with no minimum quantities

- Volume discounts available for bulk orders of 50+ copies

You provide the expertise – let us provide the materials

Contact *sales@testprepworks.com* for more info

1 - Setup fees start at $199 per title, which includes branding of the cover and title page and a customer-provided introductory message. Additional customization will incur additional setup fees.

2 - The list price for custom books is the same as the list price of the corresponding title available for retail sale. If the content of a book is modified so that it no longer corresponds to a book available for retail sale, then Test Prep Works will set the list price prior to assessing any setup fees.

TEST PREP WORKS, LLC.

THE BEST *Unofficial* PRACTICE TESTS FOR THE Upper Level SSAT

TEST PREP WORKS, LLC • **CHRISTA ABBOTT, M.ED.**

Published by:
Test Prep Works, LLC
PO Box 100572
Arlington, VA 22210
www.TestPrepWorks.com

For information about buying this title in bulk, or for editions with customized covers or content, please contact the publisher at sales@testprepworks.com or (703) 944-6727.

The SSAT is a registered trademark of The Enrollment Management Association, which has neither endorsed nor associated itself in any way with this book.

Neither the author nor the publisher of this book claims responsibility for the accuracy of this book or the outcome of students who use these materials.

ISBN: 978-1-68059-002-9

Contents

How To Use This Book

The tests in this book will give you an idea of the types of questions you will see, the concepts that are being tested, and the format and timing of the test. You will also get a sense of how the scoring works – one point is given for correct answers and a quarter point is subtracted for incorrect answers.

Try to work through the test in "real conditions" to get a sense of what it feels like to take a test of this length, which may be longer than what you are used to. Be sure to time yourself on each section and stop when the time is up, just like you will have to on test day.

The following chart lays out the general timing of the test:

Section	Time
Writing Sample – choose 1 prompt	25 minutes
*** 5 Minute Break ***	
1st Quantitative Section – 25 questions	30 minutes
Reading Section – 40 questions	40 minutes
*** 10 Minute Break ***	
Verbal Section – 60 questions	30 minutes
2nd Quantitative Section – 25 questions	30 minutes

There may also be a 15-minute experimental section at the end of the actual test. These questions will NOT contribute to your score. The test writers are simply trying out new questions for a future SSAT.

After you complete Practice Test 1, check all of your answers. Figure out WHY you missed the questions that you answered incorrectly. Then, think about what you would do differently BEFORE you start Practice Test 2.

About Test Prep Works, LLC

Test Prep Works, LLC, was founded to provide effective materials for test preparation. Its founder, Christa Abbott, spent years looking for effective materials for the private school entrance exams but came up empty-handed. The books available combined several different tests and while there are overlaps, they are not the same test. Christa found this to be overwhelming for students who were in Elementary and Middle School and that just didn't seem necessary. Christa developed her own materials to use with students that are specific for each level of the test and are not just adapted from other books. Now, these materials are available to the general public as well as other tutors. Please visit www.TestPrepWorks.com to view a complete array of offerings as well as sign up for a newsletter with recent news and developments in the world of admissions and test preparation.

Answer Sheets

The following pages contain answer sheets for each of the two practice tests. Additional copies can be downloaded at:

www.testprepworks.com/student/download

Practice Test 1

Section 1: Quantitative

1 (A) (B) (C) (D) (E)
2 (A) (B) (C) (D) (E)
3 (A) (B) (C) (D) (E)
4 (A) (B) (C) (D) (E)
5 (A) (B) (C) (D) (E)
6 (A) (B) (C) (D) (E)
7 (A) (B) (C) (D) (E)
8 (A) (B) (C) (D) (E)
9 (A) (B) (C) (D) (E)
10 (A) (B) (C) (D) (E)
11 (A) (B) (C) (D) (E)
12 (A) (B) (C) (D) (E)
13 (A) (B) (C) (D) (E)
14 (A) (B) (C) (D) (E)
15 (A) (B) (C) (D) (E)
16 (A) (B) (C) (D) (E)
17 (A) (B) (C) (D) (E)
18 (A) (B) (C) (D) (E)
19 (A) (B) (C) (D) (E)
20 (A) (B) (C) (D) (E)
21 (A) (B) (C) (D) (E)
22 (A) (B) (C) (D) (E)
23 (A) (B) (C) (D) (E)
24 (A) (B) (C) (D) (E)
25 (A) (B) (C) (D) (E)

Section 2: Reading Comprehension

1 (A) (B) (C) (D) (E)
2 (A) (B) (C) (D) (E)
3 (A) (B) (C) (D) (E)
4 (A) (B) (C) (D) (E)
5 (A) (B) (C) (D) (E)
6 (A) (B) (C) (D) (E)
7 (A) (B) (C) (D) (E)
8 (A) (B) (C) (D) (E)
9 (A) (B) (C) (D) (E)
10 (A) (B) (C) (D) (E)
11 (A) (B) (C) (D) (E)
12 (A) (B) (C) (D) (E)
13 (A) (B) (C) (D) (E)
14 (A) (B) (C) (D) (E)
15 (A) (B) (C) (D) (E)
16 (A) (B) (C) (D) (E)
17 (A) (B) (C) (D) (E)
18 (A) (B) (C) (D) (E)
19 (A) (B) (C) (D) (E)
20 (A) (B) (C) (D) (E)
21 (A) (B) (C) (D) (E)
22 (A) (B) (C) (D) (E)
23 (A) (B) (C) (D) (E)
24 (A) (B) (C) (D) (E)
25 (A) (B) (C) (D) (E)
26 (A) (B) (C) (D) (E)
27 (A) (B) (C) (D) (E)
28 (A) (B) (C) (D) (E)
29 (A) (B) (C) (D) (E)
30 (A) (B) (C) (D) (E)
31 (A) (B) (C) (D) (E)
32 (A) (B) (C) (D) (E)
33 (A) (B) (C) (D) (E)
34 (A) (B) (C) (D) (E)
35 (A) (B) (C) (D) (E)
36 (A) (B) (C) (D) (E)
37 (A) (B) (C) (D) (E)
38 (A) (B) (C) (D) (E)
39 (A) (B) (C) (D) (E)
40 (A) (B) (C) (D) (E)

Section 3: Verbal

1 (A) (B) (C) (D) (E)	21 (A) (B) (C) (D) (E)	41 (A) (B) (C) (D) (E)
2 (A) (B) (C) (D) (E)	22 (A) (B) (C) (D) (E)	42 (A) (B) (C) (D) (E)
3 (A) (B) (C) (D) (E)	23 (A) (B) (C) (D) (E)	43 (A) (B) (C) (D) (E)
4 (A) (B) (C) (D) (E)	24 (A) (B) (C) (D) (E)	44 (A) (B) (C) (D) (E)
5 (A) (B) (C) (D) (E)	25 (A) (B) (C) (D) (E)	45 (A) (B) (C) (D) (E)
6 (A) (B) (C) (D) (E)	26 (A) (B) (C) (D) (E)	46 (A) (B) (C) (D) (E)
7 (A) (B) (C) (D) (E)	27 (A) (B) (C) (D) (E)	47 (A) (B) (C) (D) (E)
8 (A) (B) (C) (D) (E)	28 (A) (B) (C) (D) (E)	48 (A) (B) (C) (D) (E)
9 (A) (B) (C) (D) (E)	29 (A) (B) (C) (D) (E)	49 (A) (B) (C) (D) (E)
10 (A) (B) (C) (D) (E)	30 (A) (B) (C) (D) (E)	50 (A) (B) (C) (D) (E)
11 (A) (B) (C) (D) (E)	31 (A) (B) (C) (D) (E)	51 (A) (B) (C) (D) (E)
12 (A) (B) (C) (D) (E)	32 (A) (B) (C) (D) (E)	52 (A) (B) (C) (D) (E)
13 (A) (B) (C) (D) (E)	33 (A) (B) (C) (D) (E)	53 (A) (B) (C) (D) (E)
14 (A) (B) (C) (D) (E)	34 (A) (B) (C) (D) (E)	54 (A) (B) (C) (D) (E)
15 (A) (B) (C) (D) (E)	35 (A) (B) (C) (D) (E)	55 (A) (B) (C) (D) (E)
16 (A) (B) (C) (D) (E)	36 (A) (B) (C) (D) (E)	56 (A) (B) (C) (D) (E)
17 (A) (B) (C) (D) (E)	37 (A) (B) (C) (D) (E)	57 (A) (B) (C) (D) (E)
18 (A) (B) (C) (D) (E)	38 (A) (B) (C) (D) (E)	58 (A) (B) (C) (D) (E)
19 (A) (B) (C) (D) (E)	39 (A) (B) (C) (D) (E)	59 (A) (B) (C) (D) (E)
20 (A) (B) (C) (D) (E)	40 (A) (B) (C) (D) (E)	60 (A) (B) (C) (D) (E)

Section 4: Quantitative

1 (A) (B) (C) (D) (E)	10 (A) (B) (C) (D) (E)	19 (A) (B) (C) (D) (E)
2 (A) (B) (C) (D) (E)	11 (A) (B) (C) (D) (E)	20 (A) (B) (C) (D) (E)
3 (A) (B) (C) (D) (E)	12 (A) (B) (C) (D) (E)	21 (A) (B) (C) (D) (E)
4 (A) (B) (C) (D) (E)	13 (A) (B) (C) (D) (E)	22 (A) (B) (C) (D) (E)
5 (A) (B) (C) (D) (E)	14 (A) (B) (C) (D) (E)	23 (A) (B) (C) (D) (E)
6 (A) (B) (C) (D) (E)	15 (A) (B) (C) (D) (E)	24 (A) (B) (C) (D) (E)
7 (A) (B) (C) (D) (E)	16 (A) (B) (C) (D) (E)	25 (A) (B) (C) (D) (E)
8 (A) (B) (C) (D) (E)	17 (A) (B) (C) (D) (E)	
9 (A) (B) (C) (D) (E)	18 (A) (B) (C) (D) (E)	

Practice Test 2

Section 1: Quantitative

1 (A) (B) (C) (D) (E)
2 (A) (B) (C) (D) (E)
3 (A) (B) (C) (D) (E)
4 (A) (B) (C) (D) (E)
5 (A) (B) (C) (D) (E)
6 (A) (B) (C) (D) (E)
7 (A) (B) (C) (D) (E)
8 (A) (B) (C) (D) (E)
9 (A) (B) (C) (D) (E)
10 (A) (B) (C) (D) (E)
11 (A) (B) (C) (D) (E)
12 (A) (B) (C) (D) (E)
13 (A) (B) (C) (D) (E)
14 (A) (B) (C) (D) (E)
15 (A) (B) (C) (D) (E)
16 (A) (B) (C) (D) (E)
17 (A) (B) (C) (D) (E)
18 (A) (B) (C) (D) (E)
19 (A) (B) (C) (D) (E)
20 (A) (B) (C) (D) (E)
21 (A) (B) (C) (D) (E)
22 (A) (B) (C) (D) (E)
23 (A) (B) (C) (D) (E)
24 (A) (B) (C) (D) (E)
25 (A) (B) (C) (D) (E)

Section 2: Reading Comprehension

1 (A) (B) (C) (D) (E)
2 (A) (B) (C) (D) (E)
3 (A) (B) (C) (D) (E)
4 (A) (B) (C) (D) (E)
5 (A) (B) (C) (D) (E)
6 (A) (B) (C) (D) (E)
7 (A) (B) (C) (D) (E)
8 (A) (B) (C) (D) (E)
9 (A) (B) (C) (D) (E)
10 (A) (B) (C) (D) (E)
11 (A) (B) (C) (D) (E)
12 (A) (B) (C) (D) (E)
13 (A) (B) (C) (D) (E)
14 (A) (B) (C) (D) (E)
15 (A) (B) (C) (D) (E)
16 (A) (B) (C) (D) (E)
17 (A) (B) (C) (D) (E)
18 (A) (B) (C) (D) (E)
19 (A) (B) (C) (D) (E)
20 (A) (B) (C) (D) (E)
21 (A) (B) (C) (D) (E)
22 (A) (B) (C) (D) (E)
23 (A) (B) (C) (D) (E)
24 (A) (B) (C) (D) (E)
25 (A) (B) (C) (D) (E)
26 (A) (B) (C) (D) (E)
27 (A) (B) (C) (D) (E)
28 (A) (B) (C) (D) (E)
29 (A) (B) (C) (D) (E)
30 (A) (B) (C) (D) (E)
31 (A) (B) (C) (D) (E)
32 (A) (B) (C) (D) (E)
33 (A) (B) (C) (D) (E)
34 (A) (B) (C) (D) (E)
35 (A) (B) (C) (D) (E)
36 (A) (B) (C) (D) (E)
37 (A) (B) (C) (D) (E)
38 (A) (B) (C) (D) (E)
39 (A) (B) (C) (D) (E)
40 (A) (B) (C) (D) (E)

Section 3: Verbal

1 (A) (B) (C) (D) (E)	21 (A) (B) (C) (D) (E)	41 (A) (B) (C) (D) (E)
2 (A) (B) (C) (D) (E)	22 (A) (B) (C) (D) (E)	42 (A) (B) (C) (D) (E)
3 (A) (B) (C) (D) (E)	23 (A) (B) (C) (D) (E)	43 (A) (B) (C) (D) (E)
4 (A) (B) (C) (D) (E)	24 (A) (B) (C) (D) (E)	44 (A) (B) (C) (D) (E)
5 (A) (B) (C) (D) (E)	25 (A) (B) (C) (D) (E)	45 (A) (B) (C) (D) (E)
6 (A) (B) (C) (D) (E)	26 (A) (B) (C) (D) (E)	46 (A) (B) (C) (D) (E)
7 (A) (B) (C) (D) (E)	27 (A) (B) (C) (D) (E)	47 (A) (B) (C) (D) (E)
8 (A) (B) (C) (D) (E)	28 (A) (B) (C) (D) (E)	48 (A) (B) (C) (D) (E)
9 (A) (B) (C) (D) (E)	29 (A) (B) (C) (D) (E)	49 (A) (B) (C) (D) (E)
10 (A) (B) (C) (D) (E)	30 (A) (B) (C) (D) (E)	50 (A) (B) (C) (D) (E)
11 (A) (B) (C) (D) (E)	31 (A) (B) (C) (D) (E)	51 (A) (B) (C) (D) (E)
12 (A) (B) (C) (D) (E)	32 (A) (B) (C) (D) (E)	52 (A) (B) (C) (D) (E)
13 (A) (B) (C) (D) (E)	33 (A) (B) (C) (D) (E)	53 (A) (B) (C) (D) (E)
14 (A) (B) (C) (D) (E)	34 (A) (B) (C) (D) (E)	54 (A) (B) (C) (D) (E)
15 (A) (B) (C) (D) (E)	35 (A) (B) (C) (D) (E)	55 (A) (B) (C) (D) (E)
16 (A) (B) (C) (D) (E)	36 (A) (B) (C) (D) (E)	56 (A) (B) (C) (D) (E)
17 (A) (B) (C) (D) (E)	37 (A) (B) (C) (D) (E)	57 (A) (B) (C) (D) (E)
18 (A) (B) (C) (D) (E)	38 (A) (B) (C) (D) (E)	58 (A) (B) (C) (D) (E)
19 (A) (B) (C) (D) (E)	39 (A) (B) (C) (D) (E)	59 (A) (B) (C) (D) (E)
20 (A) (B) (C) (D) (E)	40 (A) (B) (C) (D) (E)	60 (A) (B) (C) (D) (E)

Section 4: Quantitative

1 (A) (B) (C) (D) (E)	10 (A) (B) (C) (D) (E)	19 (A) (B) (C) (D) (E)
2 (A) (B) (C) (D) (E)	11 (A) (B) (C) (D) (E)	20 (A) (B) (C) (D) (E)
3 (A) (B) (C) (D) (E)	12 (A) (B) (C) (D) (E)	21 (A) (B) (C) (D) (E)
4 (A) (B) (C) (D) (E)	13 (A) (B) (C) (D) (E)	22 (A) (B) (C) (D) (E)
5 (A) (B) (C) (D) (E)	14 (A) (B) (C) (D) (E)	23 (A) (B) (C) (D) (E)
6 (A) (B) (C) (D) (E)	15 (A) (B) (C) (D) (E)	24 (A) (B) (C) (D) (E)
7 (A) (B) (C) (D) (E)	16 (A) (B) (C) (D) (E)	25 (A) (B) (C) (D) (E)
8 (A) (B) (C) (D) (E)	17 (A) (B) (C) (D) (E)	
9 (A) (B) (C) (D) (E)	18 (A) (B) (C) (D) (E)	

Practice Test 1

Writing Sample

The writing sample is a way for schools to learn a little more about you. Below are two possible writing topics. Please choose the topic that you find most interesting. Fill in the circle next to the topic you chose and then use this page and the next to write your essay.

(A)   What do you think has been the most important development in science? Why?
(B)   I nervously chewed on my pencil and waited for my name to be called.

Complete your writing sample on this page and the next. You have 25 minutes to complete this section.

CONTINUE TO THE NEXT PAGE

STOP

Section 1: Quantitative

25 questions

30 minutes

Directions: Each problem is followed by five answer choices. Figure out each problem and then decide which answer choice is best.

---

1. 16, 10, 20, 5, 28, 30

   What is the median of the numbers given above?

   (A) 14

   (B) 16

   (C) 18

   (D) 20

   (E) 22

---

2. Which figure has a path that can be traveled without lifting the pencil or retracing?

   (A)

   (B)

   (C)

   (D)

   (E)

CONTINUE TO THE NEXT PAGE

3. A flooring company charges $10 per square foot for the first 100 square feet of flooring installed, and then $4 per square foot after the first 100. How much would the company charge to install 500 square feet of flooring?

    (A) $2,000
    (B) $2,100
    (C) $2,600
    (D) $3,000
    (E) $5,000

4. Snow fell every day of the week that Erika tracked. Estimate the total snowfall for the week according to the measurements in her table.

Erika's Snowfall Measurements

Day	Inches of snow
Sunday	3.8
Monday	2.1
Tuesday	8.9
Wednesday	0.2
Thursday	11.1
Friday	4.5
Saturday	2.7

    (A) 11 in
    (B) 22 in
    (C) 30 in
    (D) 34 in
    (E) 45 in

5. Sheldon has n fewer toothpicks than Mindy. If Mindy has 16 toothpicks, then how many toothpicks does Sheldon have?

    (A) $16 - n$
    (B) $16 \div n$
    (C) $n \div 16$
    (D) $n + 16$
    (E) $16n$

CONTINUE TO THE NEXT PAGE

6. A red cube has a side length of 3 *cm*. A blue cube has a base with a perimeter of 36 *cm*. How many red cubes would be needed to make a cube the same size as the blue cube?

    (A) 3
    (B) 9
    (C) 12
    (D) 27
    (E) 144

7. Which of the following is a possible value of x given the inequality?

$$x - \frac{1}{4} > \frac{3}{4}$$

    (A) $\frac{1}{4}$

    (B) $\frac{1}{2}$

    (C) $\frac{3}{4}$

    (D) 1

    (E) $1\frac{1}{4}$

8. Neil decides to sell lemonade for $0.50 per cup. If he sells 1 cup on the first day, two cups on the second day, three cups on the third day, and the pattern continues, what will his total sales be over the first 21 days?

    (A) $10.50
    (B) $115.50
    (C) $220.50
    (D) $231.00
    (E) $235.50

CONTINUE TO THE NEXT PAGE

Use the following figure for questions 9-10:

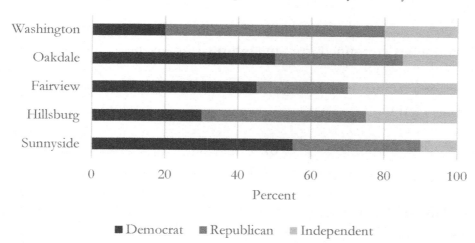

Party Affiliation of Registered Voters by County

9. Approximately what fraction of voters in Sunnyside County are registered as Republican?

(A) $\dfrac{1}{10}$

(B) $\dfrac{1}{4}$

(C) $\dfrac{7}{20}$

(D) $\dfrac{11}{20}$

(E) $\dfrac{9}{10}$

10. If there are 80,000 registered voters in Fairview County, then about how many more are registered as Democrat than Independent?

(A) 8,000

(B) 12,000

(C) 24,000

(D) 36,000

(E) 56,000

CONTINUE TO THE NEXT PAGE

11. If $M + N = 12$ and $N - 6 = P$, then what is N equal to?

   (A) 2
   (B) 3
   (C) 6
   (D) 9
   (E) Cannot be determined from the information given

12. For the calculation:

$$\frac{62,771}{892}$$

   Which of the following is closest to the result?

   (A) 70
   (B) 80
   (C) 600
   (D) 700
   (E) 800

13. A bridge has a weight limit of 5,000 kg. What is the heaviest load that a pickup truck weighing 4,500 pounds could tow across that bridge? (1 kg = 2.2 pounds)

   (A) 500 pounds
   (B) 1,100 pounds
   (C) 5,000 pounds
   (D) 6,500 pounds
   (E) 9,900 pounds

CONTINUE TO THE NEXT PAGE

14. In the following figure, the length of *DF* is 36 inches.

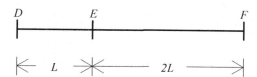

What is the length of *EF*, in inches?

(A) 30

(B) 24

(C) 18

(D) 12

(E) 6

15. What is 80% of a number if 25% of that same number is 30?

(A) 20

(B) 24

(C) 30

(D) 55

(E) 96

16. $\sqrt[3]{x^7}$

(A) x^4

(B) $\frac{1}{3}x^7$

(C) $x^2\left(\sqrt[3]{x}\right)$

(D) $\sqrt{x^{21}}$

(E) $x^{3/7}$

CONTINUE TO THE NEXT PAGE

17. The points $(6, 3)$ and $(5, n)$ are found on a line that is perpendicular to the line with the equation $y = -\frac{1}{3}x + 4$. What must be the value of n?

(A) -3

(B) $-\frac{1}{3}$

(C) 0

(D) $2\frac{2}{3}$

(E) 6

18. The figure shows a circle inscribed within a square.

If the radius of the circle is 10, then what is the area of the shaded region?

(A) $400 - 100\pi$
(B) $400 - 25\pi$
(C) $200 - 50\pi$
(D) $100 - 25\pi$
(E) 100

19. Beth purchased a television set. The television was on sale for 30% off of the original price, and Beth used a coupon that let her save an additional 10% off of the sale price. What percent of the original price did Beth pay for the television?

(A) 30%
(B) 37%
(C) 60%
(D) 63%
(E) 77%

CONTINUE TO THE NEXT PAGE

The figure shows a "T" shape made up of four smaller squares.

Which of the following figures could be created with non-overlapping "T" shapes?

(A)

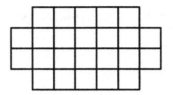

(B)

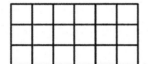

(C)

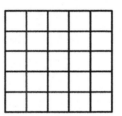

(D)

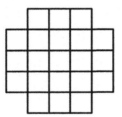

(E)

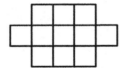

CONTINUE TO THE NEXT PAGE

21. Shari begins drawing a figure, starting at point *A* and continuing to point *B*.

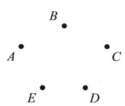

Which of the following figures could she NOT draw without lifting her pencil or retracing a line?

(A)

(B)

(C)

(D)

(E)

---

22. Which is equivalent to $6m^2 + 14m - 12$?

    (A) $(3m + 2)(2m - 6)$
    (B) $(3m - 2)(2m + 6)$
    (C) $(3m - 2)(2m - 6)$
    (D) $(6m - 2)(m + 6)$
    (E) $(6m + 2)(m - 6)$

CONTINUE TO THE NEXT PAGE

23. If d is an integer such that $2 < d < 20$, then what is the probability that 3 is a factor of d but 4 is not?

 (A) $\dfrac{5}{17}$

 (B) $\dfrac{1}{12}$

 (C) $\dfrac{1}{6}$

 (D) $\dfrac{1}{4}$

 (E) $\dfrac{1}{3}$

---

24. An amusement park averages 250 customers each day. In an effort to increase profits, the manager decides to reduce the cost of admission from $40 to $30 after 2 PM. If 175 customers pay $40 each, then how many people must buy admission after 2 PM in order to make the same amount of sales as before the change?

 (A) 75
 (B) 100
 (C) 175
 (D) 250
 (E) 333

---

25. The average of 3 consecutive odd numbers is 17. What is the largest of the 3 numbers?

 (A) 15
 (B) 16
 (C) 17
 (D) 18
 (E) 19

STOP

IF YOU HAVE TIME LEFT YOU MAY CHECK YOUR ANSWERS IN THIS SECTION ONLY

Section 2: Reading Comprehension

40 questions

40 minutes

Directions: Read each passage in this section carefully and answer the questions that follow. Choose the best answer based on the passage.

Between us there was, as I have already said somewhere, the bond of the sea. Besides holding our hearts together through long periods of separation, it had the effect of making us tolerant of each other's yarns—and even convictions. The Lawyer—the best of old fellows—had, because of his many years and many

Line 5   virtues, the only cushion on deck, and was lying on the only rug. The Accountant had brought out already a box of dominoes, and was toying architecturally with the bones. Marlow sat cross-legged right aft, leaning against the mizzen-mast. He had sunken cheeks, a yellow complexion, a straight back, an ascetic aspect, and, with his arms dropped, the palms of hands outwards, resembled an idol. The

10   director, satisfied the anchor had good hold, made his way aft and sat down amongst us. We exchanged a few words lazily. Afterwards there was silence on board the yacht. For some reason or other we did not begin that game of dominoes. We felt meditative, and fit for nothing but placid staring. The day was ending in a serenity of still and exquisite brilliance.

1. The primary purpose of this passage is to

   (A) introduce a mystery
   (B) describe early travel
   (C) provide a conclusion
   (D) describe a gathering of friends
   (E) describe weather patterns at sea

2. It can be inferred from the passage that "bones" (line 7) are

   (A) stories
   (B) dominoes
   (C) cushions
   (D) anchors
   (E) waves

3. The author's attitude toward the sea in this passage can best be described as

   (A) fear
   (B) resentment
   (C) peacefulness
   (D) indifference
   (E) disgust

CONTINUE TO THE NEXT PAGE

4. As he is described in the passage, Marlow seems to be

   (A) healthy
   (B) belligerent
   (C) mindful of others
   (D) talkative
   (E) meditative

CONTINUE TO THE NEXT PAGE

It has often been said that the greatest Frenchman who ever lived was in reality an Italian. It might with equal truth be asserted that the greatest Russian woman who ever lived was in reality a German. But the Emperor Napoleon and the Empress Catharine II resemble each other in something else. Napoleon, though Italian in blood and lineage, made himself so French in sympathy and understanding as to be able to play upon the imagination of all France as a great musician plays upon a splendid instrument, with absolute sureness of touch and an ability to extract from it every one of its varied harmonies. So the Empress Catharine of Russia—perhaps the greatest woman who ever ruled a nation—though born of German parents, became Russian to the core and made herself the embodiment of Russian feeling and Russian aspiration.

Line 5

10

Her complexion was not clear, yet her look was a very pleasing one. She had a certain diffidence of manner at first; but later she bore herself with such instinctive dignity as to make her seem majestic, though in fact she was beneath the middle size. At the time of her marriage her figure was slight and graceful; only in after years did she become stout. Altogether, she came to St. Petersburg an attractive, pure-minded German maiden, with a character well disciplined, and possessing reserves of power which had not yet been drawn upon.

15

5. It can be inferred from the passage that Napoleon

   (A) admired the French greatly
   (B) lived to old age in Italy
   (C) was good friends with Catharine II
   (D) looked a lot like Catharine II
   (E) was a ruler of Russia

6. The author implies that Catharine II

   (A) was a ruthless leader
   (B) ruled without opposition
   (C) gained weight throughout her lifetime
   (D) was proud of her Russian lineage
   (E) was idealistic as a young person

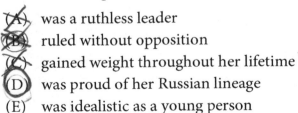

CONTINUE TO THE NEXT PAGE

7. The phrase "as a great musician plays upon a splendid instrument" (lines 6-7) is an example of

(A) personification
(B) hyperbole
(C) allegory
(D) anecdote
(E) simile

8. According to the passage, Catharine II became

(A) allied with Napoleon
(B) a hot-headed leader
(C) not important to the history of Russia
(D) a powerful ruler
(E) attractive but unreliable

9. The word "embodiment" (line 11) refers to

(A) inspiration for
(B) a perfect example
(C) a rejection of
(D) Russian morals
(E) a corpse

CONTINUE TO THE NEXT PAGE

Many people assume that the most important raw ingredient for starting a new business is a good idea. However, many brilliant ideas never become businesses because of one lacking crucial element – cash.

Line 5 In many parts of the world, the best way for citizens to lift themselves out of poverty is to create products that can be sold to the residents of wealthier nations. The issue is that capital is needed in order to get the enterprise off the ground. Raw materials need to be purchased and it takes money to handle the logistics of moving goods around the world. However, many of the families living in poverty do not have enough money to pay for basic necessities, let alone invest
10 in a new business that would be a pathway to greater prosperity.

In some cases, a person with an idea for a new company would go to a bank and get a loan to cover the startup costs. In many locations, there is no access to banks, however. There is nowhere for would-be business owners to obtain the money needed for initial investment.

15 The world of microfinancing has stepped in to fill this gap. As the name implies, microfinancing describes very small loans that are given to help a person start a business. It is important to note that these are loans and not outright gifts. Recipients are expected to repay the loans as their business grows so that more money can be extended to other entrepreneurs.

20 Many microfinancing projects focus specifically on improving the lives of women. The thought is that by improving the lives of women, small business loans will also improve the lives of the children living in these low or no income households. In this fashion, even small amounts of money can break the cycle of poverty from one generation to the next.

10. The recipients of microfinance loans most likely

(A) have a brilliant business idea
(B) don't want to go to family members for loans
(C) live in an area that lacks financial institutions
(D) don't trust traditional banks
(E) will succeed in their new business

CONTINUE TO THE NEXT PAGE

11. The word "capital" (line 6) refers to

   (A) investment money
   (B) a place of business
   (C) profit
   (D) entrepreneurs
   (E) a product

12. Which of the following would be most desirable for a microfinancing project?

   (A) building a new factory
   (B) purchasing fabric to make decorative wall hangings to sell
   (C) setting up a new rail line to deliver goods
   (D) giving food to refugees
   (E) a family constructing a new home to live in

13. It is implied in the passage that loans to women

   (A) are rarely paid back
   (B) are limited
   (C) often come from a bank
   (D) pay for child workers
   (E) affect whole families

14. The phrase "off the ground" (lines 6-7) most nearly means

   (A) lifted up
   (B) maintained
   (C) up high
   (D) successfully launched
   (E) struggling

15. The passage implies that logistics

   (A) are difficult in developing countries
   (B) limit the usefulness of microfinancing
   (C) cost money
   (D) require good ideas
   (E) stimulate growth

CONTINUE TO THE NEXT PAGE

Line 5

10

15

20

To be hopeful in an artistic sense it is not necessary to think that the world is good. It is enough to believe that there is no impossibility of its being made so. If the flight of imaginative thought may be allowed to rise superior to many moralities current amongst mankind, a novelist who would think himself of a superior essence to other men would miss the first condition of his calling. To have the gift of words is no such great matter. A man furnished with a long-range weapon does not become a hunter or a warrior by the mere possession of a fire-arm; many other qualities of character and temperament are necessary to make him either one or the other. Of him from whose armoury of phrases one in a hundred thousand may perhaps hit the far-distant and elusive mark of art I would ask that in his dealings with mankind he should be capable of giving a tender recognition to their obscure virtues. I would not have him impatient with their small failings and scornful of their errors. I would not have him expect too much gratitude from that humanity whose fate, as illustrated in individuals, it is open to him to depict as ridiculous or terrible. I would wish him to look with a large forgiveness at men's ideas and prejudices, which are by no means the outcome of malevolence, but depend on their education, their social status, even their professions. The good artist should expect no recognition of his toil and no admiration of his genius, because his toil can with difficulty be appraised and his genius cannot possibly mean anything to the illiterate who, even from the dreadful wisdom of their evoked dead, have, so far, culled nothing but inanities and platitudes.

16. The author implies that "the gift of words" (line 6)

   (A) does not guarantee literary greatness
   (B) can lead to dissatisfaction
   (C) can be taught
   (D) is widely admired
   (E) leads to fame

17. The author cautions writers against

   (A) using firearms
   (B) focusing just on their errors
   (C) being impatient
   (D) considering imagination to be better than other virtues
   (E) reading the work of other authors

CONTINUE TO THE NEXT PAGE

18. One should "look with a large forgiveness at men's ideas" (lines 15-16) because

   (A) they are not well thought out
   (B) they come from experiences and not evil
   (C) it will lead to happiness
   (D) it is important for making good art
   (E) not everyone is ridiculous

19. What is the main point of the passage?

   (A) It is better to not be hopeful.
   (B) Artists should not expect that others will recognize genius.
   (C) If an artist is not well-known it is because he has been judged harshly.
   (D) It is enough to have the gift of words to achieve fame.
   (E) Life experiences will always influence art.

20. The word "temperament" (line 8) refers to

   (A) weapons
   (B) artistic works
   (C) humanity
   (D) attention
   (E) natural disposition

CONTINUE TO THE NEXT PAGE

In the United States, about 380 billion plastic bags are used every year. It takes almost 12 million barrels of oil to produce this many plastic bags. Unfortunately, only 1 to 2 % of plastic bags used in the United States are eventually recycled. While some of the unrecycled bags wind up in a landfill,

Line 5 many of them are destined to harm wildlife. It is estimated that plastic bags kill over one million birds each year. Some birds ingest the plastic bags, which settle into the small intestine and prevent the birds from absorbing other nutrients necessary for survival. Birds can also become entangled in plastic bags and therefore unable to fly to gather food and evade predators. Many grocery stores

10 have made it a stated priority to reduce plastic bag use so that the number of tragic wildlife deaths due to plastic will be decreased.

21. This passage would likely be found in

(A) a biography
(B) a letter from one scientist to another
(C) a brochure for an environmental group
(D) a commercial for a grocery store
(E) a technical manual

22. Which of the following can be inferred from the passage?

(A) Plastic bag use is increasing.
(B) More plastic bags are used in the United States than any other country.
(C) Plastic bags are the leading cause of death for birds.
(D) The small intestine is the site of nutrient absorption in birds.
(E) Campaigns to decrease bag use have been successful.

23. This passage is primarily about

(A) the harmful effects of plastic bags
(B) the decline of bird populations
(C) the use of oil to produce plastic bags
(D) recent changes in grocery stores
(E) rapidly growing landfills

CONTINUE TO THE NEXT PAGE

24. The word "evade" (line 9) most closely means

    (A) reduce
    (B) encourage
    (C) trick
    (D) regret
    (E) escape

CONTINUE TO THE NEXT PAGE

One January day, thirty years ago, the little town of Hanover, anchored on a windy Nebraska tableland, was trying not to be blown away. A mist of fine snowflakes was curling and eddying about the cluster of low drab buildings huddled on the gray prairie, under a gray sky. The dwelling-houses were set about haphazard on the tough prairie sod; some of them looked as if they had been moved in overnight, and others as if they were straying off by themselves, headed straight for the open plain. None of them had any appearance of permanence, and the howling wind blew under them as well as over them. The main street was a deeply rutted road, now frozen hard, which ran from the squat red railway station and the grain "elevator" at the north end of the town to the lumber yard and the horse pond at the south end. On either side of this road straggled two uneven rows of wooden buildings; the general merchandise stores, the two banks, the drug store, the feed store, the saloon, the post-office. The board sidewalks were gray with trampled snow, but at two o'clock in the afternoon the shopkeepers, having come back from dinner, were keeping well behind their frosty windows. The children were all in school, and there was nobody abroad in the streets but a few rough-looking countrymen in coarse overcoats, with their long caps pulled down to their noses. Some of them had brought their wives to town, and now and then a red or a plaid shawl flashed out of one store into the shelter of another. At the hitch-bars along the street a few heavy work-horses, harnessed to farm wagons, shivered under their blankets. About the station everything was quiet, for there would not be another train in until night.

CONTINUE TO THE NEXT PAGE

25. The town of Hanover can best be described as

   (A) loud and distant
   (B) small and lonely
   (C) rural and thriving
   (D) bucolic but sophisticated
   (E) hilly and well-built

26. The word "haphazard" (line 5) most nearly means

   (A) carelessly
   (B) cold
   (C) orderly
   (D) pleasantly
   (E) enviously

27. The phrase "straying off by themselves" (line 6) is an example of

   (A) alliteration
   (B) hyperbole
   (C) personification
   (D) metaphor
   (E) connotation

28. The general mood of this passage can best be described as

   (A) indifferent
   (B) optimistic
   (C) ironic
   (D) dispirited
   (E) forgiving

29. Where would this passage most likely be found?

   (A) a reference book
   (B) a novel
   (C) a personal diary entry
   (D) a newspaper
   (E) a scholarly journal

CONTINUE TO THE NEXT PAGE

Encamping near a spring by the side of a hill, we resumed our journey in the morning, and early in the afternoon had arrived within a few miles of Fort Leavenworth. The road crossed a stream densely bordered with trees, and running in the bottom of a deep woody hollow. We were about to descend into

Line 5 it, when a wild and confused procession appeared, passing through the water below, and coming up the steep ascent toward us. We stopped to let them pass. They were Delawares, just returned from a hunting expedition. All, both men and women, were mounted on horseback, and drove along with them a considerable number of pack mules, laden with the furs they had taken, together with the

10 buffalo robes, kettles, and other articles of their traveling equipment, which as well as their clothing and their weapons, had a worn and dingy aspect, as if they had seen hard service of late.

30. It can be inferred from the passage that in the Delaware tribe

(A)   men did all the hunting
(B)   women were in charge of hunting
(C)   hides were discarded after a hunting expedition
(D)   meat was shared with other travelers
(E)   both men and women travelled on hunting trips

31. Which of the following conclusions could be drawn from the passage?

(A)   The Delaware tribe was experiencing hard times.
(B)   The road to Fort Leavenworth was frequently busy.
(C)   Buffalo hides were extremely valuable.
(D)   The author preferred to remain hidden.
(E)   The passage occurs during wintertime.

32. According to the passage

(A)   horses were used for carrying goods
(B)   the Delaware tribal people rode mule trains
(C)   the author's group was frightened by the Delaware hunters
(D)   the Delaware tribe carried their goods with them on hunting trips
(E)   buffalo hides were hard to find

CONTINUE TO THE NEXT PAGE

33. The tone of this passage can best be described as

(A) skeptical
(B) informative
(C) flustered
(D) lackadaisical
(E) critical

CONTINUE TO THE NEXT PAGE

The fundamental fact in all ranges of life from the lowest to the highest is *activity, doing*. Every individual, either animal or man, is constantly meeting situations which demand response. In the lower forms of life, this response is very simple, while in the higher forms, and especially in man, it is very complex. The bird sees a nook favorable for a nest, and at once appropriates it; a man sees a house that strikes his fancy, and works and plans and saves for months to secure money with which to buy it. It is evident that the larger the possible number of responses, and the greater their diversity and complexity, the more difficult it will be to select and compel the right response to any given situation. Man therefore needs some special power of control over his acts—he requires a *will*.

There has been much discussion and not a little controversy as to the true nature of the will. Just what *is* the will, and what is the content of our mental stream when we are in the act of willing? Is there at such times a new and distinctly different content which we do not find in our processes of knowledge or emotion—such as perception, memory, judgment, interest, desire? Or do we find, when we are engaged in an act of the will, that the mental stream contains only the familiar old elements of attention, perception, judgment, desire, purpose, etc., *all organized or set for the purpose of accomplishing or preventing some act*?

34. The author's primary purpose is to

   (A) explain the difference between a bird and a human
   (B) describe how to fulfill a long term goal
   (C) pose a question about the nature of human will
   (D) provide background history for a complex question
   (E) illustrate examples of will

35. The author would most likely agree that a key difference between birds and man is

   (A) birds have a more advanced response
   (B) birds are more diverse
   (C) we can't know what birds are thinking
   (D) man has a more automatic response
   (E) man's ability to plan for an extended period of time

CONTINUE TO THE NEXT PAGE

36. What is the central question being posed by the author?

    (A) How does man make a decision?
    (B) Does man use familiar elements of thought directed towards a new goal?
    (C) How has thinking changed over time?
    (D) How do we decide between different responses?
    (E) Does human will exist?

37. According to the author, what is the primary purpose of human will?

    (A) to figure out different possible responses
    (B) to pay attention
    (C) to build man's skills of perception
    (D) to achieve a goal or stop something from happening
    (E) to set us apart from other animals

CONTINUE TO THE NEXT PAGE

Line 5

> The soil is gravel, peculiarly bad for roses; and at no distant day my garden was a swamp, not unchronicled had we room to dwell on such matters. The bit of lawn looked decent only at midsummer. I first tackled the rose question. The bushes and standards, such as they were, faced south, of course—that is, behind the house. A line of fruit trees there began to shade them grievously. Experts assured me that if I raised a bank against these, of such a height as I proposed, they would surely die; I paid no attention to the experts, nor did my fruit trees.

38. The writer's response to the "experts" is one of

   (A) defiance
   (B) admiration
   (C) reverence
   (D) empathy
   (E) disgust

39. Which of the following can be inferred from the passage?

   (A) The author is not an effective gardener.
   (B) The author is constantly reinventing his garden.
   (C) The branches of the fruit tree effectively block the sun.
   (D) The author's lawn is a source of pride.
   (E) Gravel should be mixed into the soil to support roses.

40. What does the author mean when he writes "at no distant day my garden was a swamp"?

   (A) The author's garden is frequently flooded when it rains.
   (B) In the near past the author's garden was a wetland.
   (C) The author expects his garden to turn into a marsh shortly.
   (D) The author has added gravel to counteract the water in his garden.
   (E) Roses prefer wet soil.

STOP

IF YOU HAVE TIME LEFT YOU MAY CHECK YOUR ANSWERS IN THIS SECTION ONLY

Section 3: Verbal

60 questions
30 minutes

This section has two types of questions- synonyms and analogies.

Synonyms

Directions: Each question has a word in all capital letters and then five answer choices that are in lower case letters. You need to choose the answer choice that has the word (or phrase) that is closest in meaning to the word that is in capital letters.

1. COMMEMORATE:

   (A) terrify
   (B) honor
   (C) limit
   (D) descend
   (E) sacrifice

2. DOCTRINE:

   (A) belief
   (B) promotion
   (C) combination
   (D) recollection
   (E) monarch

3. SANCTION:

   (A) profit
   (B) refuse
   (C) migrate
   (D) crunch
   (E) approve

CONTINUE TO THE NEXT PAGE

4. DEVOID:

    (A) enveloped

    (B) misplaced

    (C) absurd

    (D) lacking

    (E) languid

5. PARIAH:

    (A) remedy

    (B) doubt

    (C) total outcast

    (D) drudgery

    (E) small portion

6. PUNCTUAL:

    (A) on time

    (B) victorious

    (C) effortless

    (D) ridiculous

    (E) stern

7. OSTENTATIOUS:

    (A) unique

    (B) taboo

    (C) showy

    (D) innocent

    (E) darling

8. SYMPATHY:

    (A) apathy

    (B) compassion

    (C) pastime

    (D) preference

    (E) selection

CONTINUE TO THE NEXT PAGE

9. RUSE:

   (A) process
   (B) galley
   (C) motto
   (D) glee
   (E) trick

10. OVERBEARING:

   (A) counterfeit
   (B) subordinate
   (C) drowsy
   (D) domineering
   (E) scholarly

11. GAUNT:

   (A) faded
   (B) scrawny
   (C) ready
   (D) rugged
   (E) huddled

12. MISFORTUNE:

   (A) bad luck
   (B) absolute solitude
   (C) impulsive buy
   (D) primary reason
   (E) powerful ruler

13. REVOKE:

   (A) register
   (B) rally
   (C) rumble
   (D) risk
   (E) recall

CONTINUE TO THE NEXT PAGE

14. JUDICIOUS:

    (A) derelict

    (B) cranky

    (C) responsible

    (D) intruding

    (E) favorable

15. NAÏVE:

    (A) unsophisticated

    (B) curious

    (C) improved

    (D) gradual

    (E) slender

16. FABRICATE:

    (A) leave out

    (B) not accept

    (C) come again

    (D) make up

    (E) let up

17. INDETERMINATE:

    (A) easy

    (B) vague

    (C) morbid

    (D) weary

    (E) delayed

18. HACKNEYED:

    (A) overused

    (B) superlative

    (C) religious

    (D) efficient

    (E) invalid

CONTINUE TO THE NEXT PAGE

19. INSINUATE:

  (A) stubbornly refuse
  (B) graciously decline
  (C) completely devour
  (D) effortlessly finish
  (E) slyly suggest

20. FOREBODING:

  (A) immediate emergency
  (B) fleeting thought
  (C) uneasy prediction
  (D) sharp remark
  (E) traditional tale

21. SNICKER:

  (A) cheerful greeting
  (B) bored yawn
  (C) regular request
  (D) disrespectful laugh
  (E) abrupt dismissal

22. BOGUS:

  (A) pilfered
  (B) fake
  (C) sincere
  (D) corresponding
  (E) separate

23. CONTORTION:

  (A) twisting
  (B) nobility
  (C) junction
  (D) custom
  (E) abundance

CONTINUE TO THE NEXT PAGE

24. PROPAGATE:

   (A) malign
   (B) cradle
   (C) grow
   (D) demonstrate
   (E) ridicule

25. CONCOCT:

   (A) diminish
   (B) recover
   (C) replace
   (D) redress
   (E) devise

26. DUPLICITY:

   (A) mania
   (B) deceit
   (C) recreation
   (D) drudgery
   (E) severity

27. ILLEGITIMATE:

   (A) embraced
   (B) visible
   (C) patient
   (D) not genuine
   (E) ethereal

28. VERNACULAR:

   (A) language
   (B) descendant
   (C) exaggeration
   (D) script
   (E) disorder

CONTINUE TO THE NEXT PAGE

29. QUELL:

  (A) define
  (B) witness
  (C) defeat
  (D) build
  (E) counsel

30. UPBRAID:

  (A) ditch
  (B) reprimand
  (C) scrape
  (D) transport
  (E) wither

CONTINUE TO THE NEXT PAGE

Analogies

Directions: Analogies questions ask you to identify the relationship between words. Choose the answer choice that best finishes the sentence.

31. Bottle is to liquids as

    (A) plate is to fork
    (B) napkin is to placemat
    (C) bowl is to soup
    (D) cream is to milk
    (E) cup is to mug

32. Flour is to bread as

    (A) syrup is to pancake
    (B) boot is to footwear
    (C) rice is to pan
    (D) bakery is to kitchen
    (E) leather is to shoe

33. Cartography is to maps as

    (A) architecture is to blueprints
    (B) essays is to writing
    (C) masonry is to castles
    (D) photography is to vision
    (E) carpentry is to strength

34. Immeasurable is to size as

    (A) champion is to sport
    (B) ultimate is to maximum
    (C) celebration is to sound
    (D) ravenous is to hunger
    (E) infallible is to height

CONTINUE TO THE NEXT PAGE

35. Policeman is to ticket as teacher is to

   (A)   classroom
   (B)   detention
   (C)   lecture
   (D)   quiz
   (E)   textbook

36. Miner is to steelworker as

   (A)   rancher is to butcher
   (B)   painter is to photographer
   (C)   driver is to pilot
   (D)   astronomer is to physicist
   (E)   chef is to cashier

37. Walk is to gallop as

   (A)   jump is to dive
   (B)   drift is to glide
   (C)   mumble is to yell
   (D)   decelerate is to slow
   (E)   plummet is to fall

38. Cacophonous is to raucous as gregarious is to

   (A)   flippant
   (B)   sociable
   (C)   garish
   (D)   gullible
   (E)   reclusive

39. Thermometer is to heat as

   (A)   speedometer is to distance
   (B)   barometer is to rainfall
   (C)   protractor is to length
   (D)   compass is to altitude
   (E)   balance is to weight

CONTINUE TO THE NEXT PAGE

40. Dilapidated is to used as

    (A) damp is to flooded
    (B) angry is to upset
    (C) speedy is to fast
    (D) scorching is to warm
    (E) dilated is to visible

41. Vehicle is to transportation as

    (A) jacket is to clothing
    (B) stove is to cooking
    (C) desk is to office
    (D) table is to floor
    (E) medicine is to vaccination

42. Terminate is to job as

    (A) renovate is to house
    (B) accelerate is to car
    (C) register is to city
    (D) baptize is to church
    (E) expel is to school

43. Endangered is to extinct as rare is to

    (A) threatened
    (B) unique
    (C) nonexistent
    (D) unusual
    (E) dangerous

44. Poetry is to sonnet as prose is to

    (A) ode
    (B) haiku
    (C) sonata
    (D) aria
    (E) essay

CONTINUE TO THE NEXT PAGE

45. Lucrative is to profitable as

   (A)   variable is to consistent
   (B)   excruciating is to tolerable
   (C)   jocular is to athletic
   (D)   exorbitant is to excessive
   (E)   vivacious is to astute

46. Litigation is to attorneys as

   (A)   lawmaking is to legislators
   (B)   teachers is to educators
   (C)   confirmation is to veto
   (D)   construction is to machinery
   (E)   reincarnation is to ministers

47. Miff is to exasperate as

   (A)   laugh is to guffaw
   (B)   ignore is to devastate
   (C)   recuperate is to recover
   (D)   distort is to absolve
   (E)   diagnose is to cure

48. Mediation is to disagreement as

   (A)   navigation is to route
   (B)   nationalization is to conflict
   (C)   nomination is to appointment
   (D)   notation is to contract
   (E)   negotiation is to dispute

49. Pandemonium is to disorder as

   (A)   posterity is to wealth
   (B)   ecstasy is to happiness
   (C)   energy is to petroleum
   (D)   conformity is to chaos
   (E)   despair is to weeping

CONTINUE TO THE NEXT PAGE

50. Eloquent is to speaker as

    (A)   intelligent is to doctor
    (B)   patient is to teacher
    (C)   technical is to writer
    (D)   humorous is to comedian
    (E)   determined is to runner

51. Vaccine is to disease as coolant is to

    (A)   overcoming
    (B)   overhauling
    (C)   overheating
    (D)   overlaying
    (E)   overdoing

52. Absolution is to forgiveness as

    (A)   notion is to proof
    (B)   ammunition is to fray
    (C)   perception is to ignorance
    (D)   retribution is to punishment
    (E)   inception is to conclusion

53. Sill is to window as

    (A)   pane is to glass
    (B)   crank is to casement
    (C)   hearthstone is to fireplace
    (D)   kitchen is to house
    (E)   ignition is to engine

54. Episode is to show as

    (A)   epic is to summary
    (B)   script is to scene
    (C)   clarinet is to woodwind
    (D)   act is to play
    (E)   painting is to museum

CONTINUE TO THE NEXT PAGE

55. Interest is to fascinate as

    (A)   notify is to inform
    (B)   scare is to petrify
    (C)   acquire is to obtain
    (D)   transport is to move
    (E)   magnify is to enlarge

56. Wilt is to wither as

    (A)   regret is to despair
    (B)   grow is to trim
    (C)   lettuce is to plant
    (D)   trash is to criticize
    (E)   former is to latter

57. Opulent is to dining room as

    (A)   large is to basement
    (B)   short is to story
    (C)   euphonious is to melody
    (D)   flashy is to clothing
    (E)   favorable is to limousine

58. Kindred is to estranged as

    (A)   lengthen is to twist
    (B)   upbraid is to insult
    (C)   divulge is to reveal
    (D)   discreet is to tactful
    (E)   lamentable is to celebrated

59. Receipt is to acknowledgement as

    (A)   applause is to praise
    (B)   goods is to store
    (C)   shift is to work
    (D)   page is to book
    (E)   release is to confinement

CONTINUE TO THE NEXT PAGE

60. Lumber is to foot as

   (A) length is to width
   (B) milk is to cup
   (C) saw is to cut
   (D) calculation is to figure
   (E) wood is to board

STOP

IF YOU HAVE TIME LEFT YOU MAY CHECK YOUR ANSWERS IN THIS SECTION ONLY

Section 4: Quantitative

25 questions

30 minutes

Directions: Each problem is followed by five answer choices. Figure out each problem and then decide which answer choice is best.

---

1. Two numbers have a difference of 5. They also add up to 31. What is the larger of the numbers?

   (A) 13
   (B) 14
   (C) 16
   (D) 18
   (E) 23

---

2. Solve: $100 - 13\frac{11}{12}$

   (A) $86\frac{1}{12}$

   (B) $86\frac{11}{12}$

   (C) 87

   (D) $87\frac{1}{12}$

   (E) $87\frac{11}{12}$

CONTINUE TO THE NEXT PAGE

3. The distance around a hog pen is 18 yds. If fencing comes in 2 foot lengths, how many lengths of fencing will be needed to go all the way around the hog pen?

   (A) 9
   (B) 18
   (C) 27
   (D) 36
   (E) 54

4. If $12 + 2x - 4 = 4x$, then what is the value of x?

   (A) 2
   (B) 4
   (C) 6
   (D) 9
   (E) 12

5. $10.00 \times 0.0020 =$

   (A) 0.002
   (B) 0.02
   (C) 0.2
   (D) 2.0
   (E) 20

6. What is the quotient of 12.8 and 0.16?

   (A) $\dfrac{1}{800}$

   (B) $\dfrac{1}{80}$

   (C) $\dfrac{1}{8}$

   (D) 8

   (E) 80

CONTINUE TO THE NEXT PAGE

7. On his first four tests, Harry had an average score of 82. He then took a fifth test and received a score of 90 on the fifth test. What is his average for all five tests?

   (A) 81
   (B) 82
   (C) 83
   (D) 83.6
   (E) 86

8. If $M < 5$, then $4M + 2$ could be equal to

   (A) 21
   (B) 22
   (C) 23
   (D) 24
   (E) 25

9. Which of the following is NOT equivalent to $1 \times \frac{1}{5}$?

   (A) $2 \times \dfrac{1}{10}$

   (B) $3 \times \dfrac{1}{15}$

   (C) $4 \times \dfrac{2}{40}$

   (D) $5 \times \dfrac{5}{125}$

   (E) $6 \times \dfrac{1}{35}$

CONTINUE TO THE NEXT PAGE

10. The greatest of four consecutive integers is equal to five less than three times the smallest of these integers. What is the value of the greatest of these consecutive integers?

   (A) −4
   (B) 2
   (C) 4
   (D) 6
   (E) 7

---

11. One piece of candy weighs 42 mg. How many grams would 200 pieces of this candy weigh?

   (A) 7.4
   (B) 8.4
   (C) 74
   (D) 84.4
   (E) 8,400

---

12. Factor: $x^2 - 2x - 48$

   (A) $(x + 6)(x - 8)$
   (B) $(x - 6)(x + 8)$
   (C) $(x - 6)(x - 8)$
   (D) $(x - 12)(x + 4)$
   (E) $(x + 12)(x - 4)$

---

13. It took Carla between $4\frac{1}{2}$ and $5\frac{1}{2}$ hours to drive 300 miles. Her average speed, given in miles per hour, was

   (A) between 36 and 47
   (B) between 47 and 54
   (C) between 54 and 67
   (D) between 67 and 73
   (E) between 73 and 80

CONTINUE TO THE NEXT PAGE

Tim keeps track of how he spends his time over a 10-day period. Questions 14-15 refer to the graph he made with his observations.

How Tim Spent His Time (hours)

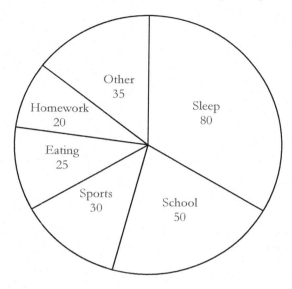

14. What portion of Tim's time is spent sleeping?

(A) $\frac{1}{6}$

(B) $\frac{1}{5}$

(C) $\frac{1}{4}$

(D) $\frac{1}{3}$

(E) $\frac{1}{2}$

15. How much time does Tim spend at school and eating, as a percentage of the time Tim spends playing sports and doing homework?

(A) 31.25%

(B) 60%

(C) 75%

(D) 120%

(E) 150%

CONTINUE TO THE NEXT PAGE

16. Simplify: $(4y^3 + 3y + 6) - (2y^2 - 5y - 5)$

    (A) $4y^3 - 2y^2 - 2y + 1$
    (B) $4y^3 - 2y^2 + 8y + 11$
    (C) $4y^3 - 2y^2 + y + 1$
    (D) $4y^3 - 2y^2 + y + 11$
    (E) $4y^3 + 2y^2 + y + 1$

17. $90 - 40(6) + 30 \div 2 =$

    (A) -135
    (B) -60
    (C) 60
    (D) 135
    (E) 270

18. $\dfrac{9a^{-2}b}{6c^{-4}d^3}$ is equivalent to

    (A) $3a^2bc^4d^3$

    (B) $\dfrac{3bc^4}{a^2d^3}$

    (C) $\dfrac{1}{3} \times \dfrac{bc^4}{a^2d^3}$

    (D) $\dfrac{2bc^4}{3a^2d^3}$

    (E) $\dfrac{3bc^4}{2a^2d^3}$

19. How many cubes that are 1 cm on each side are needed to build a larger cube that has a base perimeter of 20 cm?

    (A)   4
    (B)   5
    (C)   25
    (D)   75
    (E)   125

CONTINUE TO THE NEXT PAGE

20. $962 \div 7 =$

    (A) $\dfrac{9,000}{7} + \dfrac{600}{2} + \dfrac{70}{7} + \dfrac{2}{7}$

    (B) $\dfrac{900}{7} \times \dfrac{600}{2} \times \dfrac{70}{7} \times \dfrac{2}{7}$

    (C) $\dfrac{9}{7} + \dfrac{6}{2} + \dfrac{7}{7} + \dfrac{2}{7}$

    (D) $\dfrac{900}{7} + \dfrac{60}{7} + \dfrac{2}{7}$

    (E) $\dfrac{900}{7} \times \dfrac{60}{7} \times \dfrac{2}{7}$

---

21. Holly polled 400 students in her school who had at least one sibling. If 250 students said they had at least one sister and 325 students said that they had at least one brother, then how many students had at least one sister and at least one brother?

    (A) 75
    (B) 125
    (C) 150
    (D) 175
    (E) 225

---

22. A solid cylinder with a base diameter of 4 and a height of 6 is placed within a box. The box is a rectangular prism with a height of 6 and a square base with a side length of 4. What is the volume of the empty space in the box surrounding the cylinder?

    (A) $24 - 4\pi$
    (B) $24 - 6\pi$
    (C) $24\pi - 36$
    (D) $96 - 24\pi$
    (E) $96 - 144\pi$

CONTINUE TO THE NEXT PAGE

23. If $w < 0$, then which of the following would be greatest?

(A) $\frac{w}{w} - 1$

(B) w^3

(C) $w^3 - 1$

(D) w^5

(E) $w^5 - 1$

24. In the following figure, M is the center of the circle, angle OMN is a right angle, and points N and O are both on the circle and vertices of the triangle MNO.

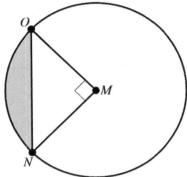

What is the area of the shaded region if the diameter of the circle is 16?

(A) 4

(B) 64

(C) $16\pi - 32$

(D) $64\pi - 128$

(E) $256\pi - 512$

25. Which answer choice is equivalent to $\frac{25x^3yz^4}{30x^2y^2z^4}$?

(A) $\frac{x}{y}$

(B) $\frac{5xz^4}{6y}$

(C) $\frac{5x}{6y}$

(D) $\frac{5x}{6yz^4}$

(E) $\frac{5z^4}{6y}$

STOP

IF YOU HAVE TIME LEFT YOU MAY CHECK YOUR ANSWERS IN THIS SECTION ONLY

Answers to Section 1: Quantitative

Correct Answers	Your Answers	Answered Correctly	Answered Incorrectly	Omitted
1. C				
2. B				
3. C				
4. D				
5. A				
6. D				
7. E				
8. B				
9. C				
10. B				
11. E				
12. A				
13. D				
14. B				
15. E				
16. C				
17. C				
18. A				
19. D				
20. A				
21. E				
22. B				
23. A				
24. B				
25. E				
Total				

Raw score = Total # answered correctly _____ – total # answered incorrectly _____ ÷ 4

Your raw score: _____

Answers to Section 2: Reading Comprehension

Correct Answers	Your Answers	Answered Correctly	Answered Incorrectly	Omitted
1. D				
2. B				
3. C				
4. E				
5. A				
6. C				
7. E				
8. D				
9. B				
10. C				
11. A				
12. B				
13. E				
14. D				
15. C				
16. A				
17. D				
18. B				
19. B				
20. E				
21. C				
22. D				
23. A				
24. E				
25. B				
26. A				
27. C				
28. D				
29. B				
30. E				
31. A				
32. D				

33. B				
34. C				
35. E				
36. B				
37. D				
38. A				
39. C				
40. B				
Total				

Raw score = Total # answered correctly _____ – total # answered incorrectly _____ ÷ 4

Your raw score: _____

Answers to Section 3: Verbal

Correct Answer	Your Answer	Answered Correctly	Answered Incorrectly	Omitted
1. B				
2. A				
3. E				
4. D				
5. C				
6. A				
7. C				
8. B				
9. E				
10. D				
11. B				
12. A				
13. E				
14. C				
15. A				
16. D				
17. B				
18. A				
19. E				
20. C				
21. D				
22. B				
23. A				
24. C				
25. E				
26. B				
27. D				
28. A				
29. C				
30. B				
31. C				
32. E				

33. A				
34. D				
35. B				
36. A				
37. C				
38. B				
39. E				
40. D				
41. B				
42. E				
43. C				
44. E				
45. D				
46. A				
47. A				
48. E				
49. B				
50. D				
51. C				
52. D				
53. C				
54. D				
55. B				
56. A				
57. D				
58. E				
59. A				
60. B				
Total				

Raw score = Total # answered correctly _____ – total # answered incorrectly _____ ÷ 4

Your raw score: _____

Answers to Section 4: Quantitative

Correct Answers	Your Answers	Answered Correctly	Answered Incorrectly	Omitted
1. D				
2. A				
3. C				
4. B				
5. B				
6. E				
7. D				
8. A				
9. E				
10. E				
11. B				
12. A				
13. C				
14. D				
15. E				
16. B				
17. A				
18. E				
19. E				
20. D				
21. D				
22. D				
23. A				
24. C				
25. C				
Total				

Raw score = Total # answered correctly _____ – total # answered incorrectly _____ ÷ 4

Your raw score: _____

Practice Test 2

Writing Sample

The writing sample is a way for schools to learn a little more about you. Below are two possible writing topics. Please choose the topic that you find most interesting. Fill in the circle next to the topic you chose and then use this page and the next to write your essay.

(A) If you could go back in time and witness one historical event, which would it be? Why?

(B) That summer was the hottest on record.

Complete your writing sample on this page and the next. You have 25 minutes to complete this section.

CONTINUE TO THE NEXT PAGE

Practice Test 2

73

STOP

Section 1: Quantitative

25 questions

30 minutes

Directions: Each problem is followed by five answer choices. Figure out each problem and then decide which answer choice is best.

---

1. Sheila has saved $600. If she spends 30% of her savings on a new bicycle, how much money will she have left?

   (A) $30
   (B) $60
   (C) $180
   (D) $420
   (E) $18,000

---

2. Lorenza has green, red, yellow, and blue booklets. If she is stacking them in that order, starting with green as the 1st book in the stack, which of the following books will be yellow?

   (A) 16th
   (B) 19th
   (C) 21st
   (D) 24th
   (E) 26th

CONTINUE TO THE NEXT PAGE

3. $-\left(\dfrac{2}{3}\right)^{4} =$

   (A) $-\dfrac{16}{81}$

   (B) $-\dfrac{16}{3}$

   (C) $\dfrac{8}{3}$

   (D) $\dfrac{16}{3}$

   (E) $\dfrac{16}{81}$

---

4. Refer to the following figure for the question:

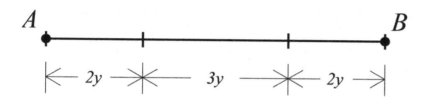

Which of the following could possibly be the length of segment AB, if y is a whole number?

   (A) 2
   (B) 3
   (C) 5
   (D) 10
   (E) 14

CONTINUE TO THE NEXT PAGE

5. Refer to the following figure for the question:

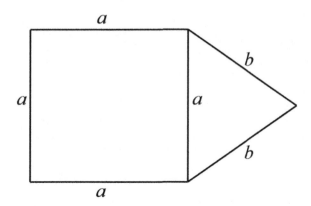

If the perimeter of the square is 48 and the perimeter of the triangle is 32, then what is $a + b$ equal to?

(A) 12
(B) 22
(C) 32
(D) 48
(E) 80

6. A team of 13 basketball players must take cars to get to its game. If each car holds a minimum of one player and a maximum of five players, and no two cars can have the same number of players, what is the smallest number of cars that can be used to transport all 13 players to the game?

(A) 2
(B) 3
(C) 4
(D) 5
(E) 13

CONTINUE TO THE NEXT PAGE

7. Refer to the following figure for the question:

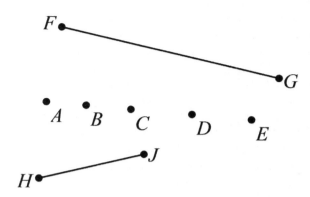

If a segment was drawn from the midpoint of segment FG to the midpoint of segment HJ, which point would be the midpoint of the newly-drawn segment?

(A) A
(B) B
(C) C
(D) D
(E) E

8. Given the inequality:

$$1 - x < \frac{2}{3}$$

x could be which of the following?

(A) $-\frac{1}{2}$

(B) $-\frac{1}{3}$

(C) 0

(D) $\frac{1}{3}$

(E) $\frac{1}{2}$

CONTINUE TO THE NEXT PAGE

9. In the following diagram, what is the measure of angle *CFE*?

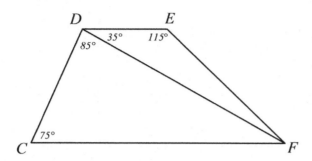

(A) 20°
(B) 30°
(C) 40°
(D) 50°
(E) 90°

10. What is the value of x in the equation $4(x - 2) + 3 = 6x$?

(A) 11

(B) 5

(C) $-\dfrac{2}{11}$

(D) $-\dfrac{2}{5}$

(E) $-\dfrac{5}{2}$

11. Myra runs 300 meters in 95 seconds on day 1 of the track season, 93 seconds on day 2, and 91 seconds on day 3. If she keeps improving at the same rate, on which day will she run 300 meters in under a minute?

(A) 19
(B) 29
(C) 39
(D) 49
(E) 59

CONTINUE TO THE NEXT PAGE

12. Refer to the following graph for the question:

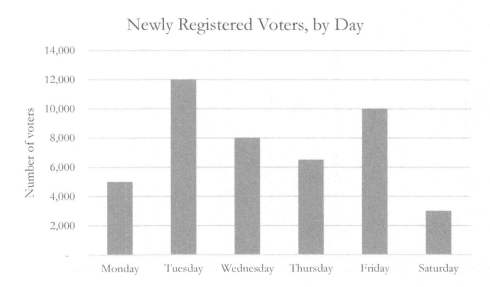

Newly Registered Voters, by Day

Which day had the largest decrease in voters registered when compared to the previous day?

(A) Tuesday
(B) Wednesday
(C) Thursday
(D) Friday
(E) Saturday

13. Which of the following is closest to the value of $\frac{61,158}{315}$?

(A) 200
(B) 300
(C) 2,000
(D) 3,000
(E) 3,043

CONTINUE TO THE NEXT PAGE

14. Refer to the following figure for the question:

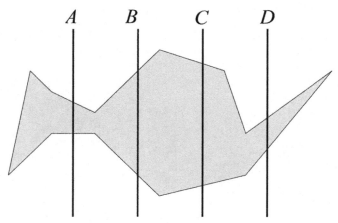

Note: This figure is not drawn to scale

The polygon shown is divided by lines *A*, *B*, *C*, and *D*. The area between *A* and *C* is 24. The area between *B* and *D* is 32. The area between *C* and *D* is 16. What is the area between *A* and *B*?

(A) 4
(B) 8
(C) 12
(D) 16
(E) 20

15. If the lengths of the first two sides of a triangle are 8 and 17, which could possibly be the length of the third side?

(A) 5
(B) 7
(C) 9
(D) 17
(E) 25

CONTINUE TO THE NEXT PAGE

16. Liam is playing a game with two made-up currencies, duros and furos. If one quarter of a duro is equal to 1.44 furos, then what must Liam multiply by 1.44 to get the value of 5 duros?

(A) $\dfrac{1}{4}$

(B) $\dfrac{1}{1.44}$

(C) 1.44

(D) 5

(E) 20

---

17. Sandy and Odie start at the same point in a field. If Sandy runs 500 meters towards his house while Odie simultaneously runs 300 meters towards his house, then how many meters apart are Sandy and Odie?

(A) 100
(B) 200
(C) 400
(D) 800
(E) Cannot be determined from the information given

---

18. Which must be true if the average of two numbers, A and B, is 75, and B is greater than A?

(A) $A + B = 75$
(B) $A - B > 75$
(C) $B - A < 75$
(D) $B - 75 = 75 - A$
(E) $B - 75 = A - 75$

---

19. 70% of n is 38. What is 35% of $2n$?

(A) 19
(B) 28
(C) 35
(D) 38
(E) 70

CONTINUE TO THE NEXT PAGE

20. The symbols ◊, □, Δ, and ◄ each represent a unique digit from 0-9. Based on the equation:

$$\begin{array}{r} \square \ \blacktriangleleft \ \Delta \\ + \ \lozenge \ \blacktriangleleft \ \Delta \\ \hline 9 \ 3 \ 0 \end{array}$$

which is a possible value for the sum of ◊ + □ + Δ + ◄?

(A) 12
(B) 15
(C) 18
(D) 21
(E) 24

---

21. Which is equivalent to $\sqrt[4]{a^8 b^9}$?

(A) $a^2 b^2 \sqrt[4]{b}$
(B) $a^2 b^2 \sqrt{b}$
(C) $a^4 b^5$
(D) $(ab)^{\frac{17}{4}}$
(E) $(ab)^{17}$

---

22. Edward has twice as many pennies as his brother. If Edward saved 50 additional pennies and his brother gave away 10, then Edward would have four times as many pennies as his brother. How many more pennies does Edward have than his brother?

(A) 10
(B) 40
(C) 45
(D) 50
(E) 105

CONTINUE TO THE NEXT PAGE

23. If the angles of a triangle measure 50°, 60°, and 70°, then what are the measures of the exterior angles of that triangle?

   (A) 20°, 30°, 40°
   (B) 50°, 60°, 70°
   (C) 80°, 90°, 100°
   (D) 110°, 120°, 130°
   (E) 290°, 300°, 310°

24. A miniature golf course charges $8.00 per customer and has an average of 250 customers each day. If the course were to lower its price to $5.00 before 4 PM, how many customers would have to pay $5.00 if 200 pay $8.00 and daily sales remain the same?

   (A) 50
   (B) 80
   (C) 120
   (D) 250
   (E) 400

25. If $f(x) = x^2 - 3x + 4$, then what is the value of $f(5) - f(3)$?

   (A) 2
   (B) 4
   (C) 8
   (D) 10
   (E) 14

STOP

IF YOU HAVE TIME LEFT YOU MAY CHECK YOUR ANSWERS IN THIS SECTION ONLY

Section 2: Reading Comprehension

40 questions

40 minutes

Directions: Read each passage in this section carefully and answer the questions that follow. Choose the best answer based on the passage.

Line 5

10

15

20

Suspicions amongst thoughts, are like bats amongst birds, they ever fly by twilight. Certainly they are to be repressed, or at least well guarded: for they cloud the mind; they leese friends; and they check with business, whereby business cannot go on currently and constantly. They dispose kings to tyranny, husbands to jealousy, wise men to irresolution and melancholy. They are defects, not in the heart, but in the brain; for they take place in the stoutest natures; as in the example of Henry the Seventh of England. There was not a more suspicious man, nor a more stout. And in such a composition they do small hurt. For commonly they are not admitted, but with examination, whether they be likely or no. But in fearful natures they gain ground too fast.

There is nothing makes a man suspect much, more than to know little; and therefore men should remedy suspicion, by procuring to know more, and not to keep their suspicions in smother. What would men have? Do they think, those they employ and deal with, are saints? Do they not think, they will have their own ends, and be truer to themselves, than to them? Therefore there is no better way, to moderate suspicions, than to account upon such suspicions as true, and yet to bridle them as false. For so far a man ought to make use of suspicions, as to provide, as if that should be true, that he suspects, yet it may do him no hurt. Suspicions that the mind of itself gathers, are but buzzes; but suspicions that are artificially nourished, and put into men's heads, by the tales and whisperings of others, have stings.

CONTINUE TO THE NEXT PAGE

1. The author writes, "There is nothing makes a man suspect much, more than to know little" (line 11). Which answer choice best expresses the author's meaning?

    (A) Men are by nature suspicious.
    (B) People are only suspicious when they have reason to be.
    (C) A lack of knowledge makes people suspicious.
    (D) Even wise men often have suspicions.
    (E) Only saints are not suspicious.

2. In line 2, the word "repressed" most nearly means

    (A) discouraged
    (B) envied
    (C) allowed
    (D) inspected
    (E) betrayed

3. The primary purpose of this passage is to

    (A) blame other people for the author's suspicions.
    (B) describe Henry the Seventh.
    (C) leave the reader in a state of suspense.
    (D) illustrate reasons for being suspicious.
    (E) explain the harm that suspicions cause.

4. What does the author suggest people do if they become suspicious?

    (A) act on their suspicions
    (B) gather more information
    (C) visit with friends
    (D) speak to wise men
    (E) listen to other people

CONTINUE TO THE NEXT PAGE

My Sorrow, when she's here with me,
Thinks these dark days of autumn rain
Are beautiful as days can be;
She loves the bare, the withered tree;
Line 5 She walks the sodden pasture lane.
Her pleasure will not let me stay.
She talks and I am fain to list:
She's glad the birds are gone away,
She's glad her simple worsted gray
10 Is silver now with clinging mist.
The desolate, deserted trees,
The faded earth, the heavy sky,
The beauties she so truly sees,
She thinks I have no eye for these,
15 And vexes me for reason why.
Not yesterday I learned to know
The love of bare November days
Before the coming of the snow,
But it were vain to tell her so,
20 And they are better for her praise.

5. Who is "she" that the speaker of the poem refers to?

(A) November days
(B) the bats that have flown away
(C) the speaker of the poem
(D) the speaker's sorrow
(E) someone who praises the speaker

6. In this poem what does the speaker author come to appreciate?

(A) how November weather makes the spring seem even better
(B) the peaceful winter snow
(C) long walks in the summer rain
(D) dreary November weather
(E) a warm fire when he returns home

CONTINUE TO THE NEXT PAGE

7. The mood of the poem can best be described as

   (A) lonely
   (B) raucous
   (C) factual
   (D) loving
   (E) exuberant

8. Which statement best summarizes the main idea of this poem?

   (A) Stay inside on cold fall days.
   (B) Always keep your socks dry.
   (C) Beauty can be found even on gray days.
   (D) People are often misunderstood.
   (E) It is hard to have a favorite season.

CONTINUE TO THE NEXT PAGE

Line 5

10

Chlorine is a commonly used gas. Because it is a strong oxidizing agent, it reacts easily with other elements and compounds. This makes it useful as a bleaching agent. It also makes it an extremely effective disinfectant in swimming pools. It is fast-acting, kills algae that might otherwise grow in pool water, and destroys contaminants such as bacteria and viruses. Its high reactivity has a downside, however, as anyone who has opened their eyes in a pool without wearing goggles can tell you.

At high concentrations, chlorine can be poisonous to humans, however. If concentrated chlorine gas enters human lungs, it can react with the water in lungs to form hydrochloric acid, which can be lethal. The first recorded instance of chlorine being used as a weapon was during World War I.

Chlorine has saved countless lives with its disinfectant properties; it has also cost many lives when used as a weapon.

9. It can be inferred from the passage that chlorine is

(A) most commonly used as a weapon
(B) is too expensive for widespread use
(C) is deadly in small doses
(D) was only discovered during World War I
(E) irritating to the human eye

10. Where would this passage most likely be found?

(A) in an anthology
(B) in a science textbook
(C) in a chemical journal
(D) in a letter between two chemists
(E) in a novel about World War I

11. The passage suggests that chlorine gas

(A) should not be released in an enclosed space
(B) is no longer used as a weapon
(C) should be banned from use
(D) is not the best disinfectant for swimming pools
(E) still needs to be further researched

CONTINUE TO THE NEXT PAGE

12. The author's tone can best be described as

    (A) angered
    (B) ambivalent
    (C) optimistic
    (D) informative
    (E) ironic

13. In line 10 the word "lethal" most nearly means

    (A) helpful
    (B) gloomy
    (C) deadly
    (D) overused
    (E) limited

14. According to the author, chlorine gas

    (A) is known in almost every country
    (B) can be both a benefit and a curse to humans
    (C) is not effective at smaller quantities
    (D) lasts a long time
    (E) is explosive at high quantities

CONTINUE TO THE NEXT PAGE

Although sharks capture the human imagination like almost no other species, we actually know relatively little about them. This is rapidly changing, however, as shark populations dwindle. There is a new urgency in learning more about sharks so that we can protect them.

Line 5   One species that scientists have been studying is thresher sharks. Thresher sharks are an unusual species. They have long, pointy tails that are almost equal in length to their entire body. Scientists have long been puzzled by their tails and why they are so long. Do thresher sharks use these tails to swim faster? Attract a potential mate? Appear more fearsome to predators?

10   A group of scientists recently decided to find out. The scientists followed a group of thresher sharks hunting in the waters off of Pescador Island in the Philippines. They carefully observed the behavior of the sharks as they attempted to feed on a school of sardines.

     The sharks were seen using their tails as a weapon. They would slap the
15 smaller sardines with their tails, leaving the sardines too stunned to move. The thresher sharks would then quickly consume the sardines before the sardines were able to recover.

     The thresher sharks were able to bring their tails in an arc through the water at an astonishing speed. The thresher sharks brought their tail down on
20 prey at an average speed of 30 miles per hour, with the fastest slap clocking in at 50 miles per hour. The sharks were also successful in stunning the prey about one-third of the times that they attempted to hunt, which is remarkable for any species.

     Now that scientists know more about how thresher sharks hunt, it will be
25 easier to put into place protections that will preserve their hunting grounds.

15. This passage is primarily concerned with

(A) different species of sharks
(B) how sardines escape thresher sharks
(C) why thresher sharks are endangered
(D) the speed with which a thresher shark can move its tail
(E) the hunting habits of thresher sharks

CONTINUE TO THE NEXT PAGE

16. According to the passage, studying thresher sharks is important because

   (A)   they are interesting

   (B)   they are one of the fastest moving species of sharks

   (C)   if we understand how they hunt we can better preserve the species

   (D)   if we can limit how often thresher sharks hunt we can save the sardines species

   (E)   humans rely on thresher sharks for food

17. The passage implies that

   (A)   most species are successful in capturing prey in less than one-third of their attempts

   (B)   thresher sharks are not easily studied

   (C)   most sharks have relatively long tails

   (D)   after years of decline, shark populations are now rebounding

   (E)   thresher sharks only eat sardines

18. What does the author mean by "appear more fearsome to predators" (line 9)?

   (A)   Thresher sharks might attempt to scare prey with their size.

   (B)   Thresher sharks are intimidating to scientists.

   (C)   Thresher sharks are currently endangered.

   (D)   A large tail might make thresher sharks less likely to become prey.

   (E)   Predators are easily scared away.

19. Why were scientists puzzled by the tails of thresher sharks?

   (A)   There was no public interest in the sharks.

   (B)   The tails of thresher sharks are unlike the tails of other shark species.

   (C)   Thresher sharks had not yet been studied.

   (D)   Overfishing had left thresher sharks endangered.

   (E)   The human appetite for thresher shark tail had grown.

20. The passage implies which of the following about sardines?

   (A)   They are endangered.

   (B)   They are abundant off the coast of Pescador Island.

   (C)   They can easily escape a thresher shark.

   (D)   Little is known about them.

   (E)   Their habitat should be preserved so that thresher sharks will continue to have a food source.

CONTINUE TO THE NEXT PAGE

Line 5

10

15

20

25

30

During these first hurries I was stupid, lying still in my cabin, which was in the steerage, and cannot describe my temper: I could ill resume the first penitence which I had so apparently trampled upon and hardened myself against: I thought the bitterness of death had been past, and that this would be nothing like the first; but when the master himself came by me, as I said just now, and said we should be all lost, I was dreadfully frighted. I got up out of my cabin and looked out; but such a dismal sight I never saw: the sea ran mountains high, and broke upon us every three or four minutes; when I could look about, I could see nothing but distress round us; two ships that rode near us, we found, had cut their masts by the board, being deep laden; and our men cried out that a ship which rode about a mile ahead of us was foundered. Two more ships, being driven from their anchors, were run out of the Roads to sea, at all adventures, and that with not a mast standing. The light ships fared the best, as not so much labouring in the sea; but two or three of them drove, and came close by us, running away with only their spritsail out before the wind.

Towards evening the mate and boatswain begged the master of our ship to let them cut away the fore-mast, which he was very unwilling to do; but the boatswain protesting to him that if he did not the ship would founder, he consented; and when they had cut away the fore-mast, the main-mast stood so loose, and shook the ship so much, they were obliged to cut that away also, and make a clear deck.

Any one may judge what a condition I must be in at all this, who was but a young sailor, and who had been in such a fright before at but a little. But if I can express at this distance the thoughts I had about me at that time, I was in tenfold more horror of mind upon account of my former convictions, and the having returned from them to the resolutions I had wickedly taken at first, than I was at death itself; and these, added to the terror of the storm, put me into such a condition that I can by no words describe it. But the worst was not come yet; the storm continued with such fury that the seamen themselves acknowledged they had never seen a worse. We had a good ship, but she was deep laden, and wallowed in the sea, so that the seamen every now and then cried out she would founder.

CONTINUE TO THE NEXT PAGE

21. The narrator can best be described as

    (A)   someone recalling being an inexperienced sailor on the deck of a ship
    (B)   a boat passenger who hid out in his cabin during a storm
    (C)   an old man being sentimental
    (D)   the captain of the ship
    (E)   an accomplished storyteller

22. The crew of the ship can best be described as

    (A)   inexperienced
    (B)   frightened
    (C)   humbled
    (D)   united
    (E)   seasick

23. The passage implies that word "founder" means

    (A)   to be damaged
    (B)   to be still
    (C)   to begin again
    (D)   to shake
    (E)   to sink

24. The primary purpose of this passage is to

    (A)   explain why the masts had to be cut away
    (B)   describe a ship that sunk in a storm
    (C)   recount one man's traumatic experience
    (D)   provide guidance on how to survive on a ship during a storm
    (E)   prove the captain's incompetence

25. The ship in this passage is

    (A)   in an isolated location
    (B)   an older ship
    (C)   a light ship
    (D)   surrounded by other boats
    (E)   foundered

CONTINUE TO THE NEXT PAGE

In 1944, The New York City Opera opened its doors. It was built on the premise that opera should be affordable to all. The New York City Opera placed itself in direct competition with the Metropolitan Opera. The Metropolitan Opera had big stars and higher ticket prices to go along with those famous names.

Line 5 The New York City Opera saved money by recruiting singers that were relatively unknown. In the process, they discovered some of the leading opera singers of the 1940s such as Martha Lipton and Hugh Thompson. Unfortunately, as soon as the talent of these singers became apparent, they were poached by the Metropolitan Opera with more generous salaries.

10 The New York City Opera broke ground with making opera accessible to the masses but they also were the first major American opera troop to feature an African American performer. In 1945, at a time when much of America remained racially segregated, African American Todd Duncan took the stage at the New York City Opera playing the role of Tonio in Pagliacci. Several other African

15 American performers followed him in short order.

The New York City Opera also made a point of performing the work of American composers. This wasn't always easy as opera was not the dominant form preferred by American composers. Many operas were written in European languages. One source of conflict among members of the Opera's board was

20 whether or not operas should be translated into and performed in English so as to be more accessible to the American audience.

Sadly, after years of innovation, the New York City Opera fell on hard times. In 2013, the company ran out of money and had to shut their doors for good. New York City lost a great cultural leader.

26. Which of the following would be the best title for this passage?

(A) Todd Duncan Makes Opera History
(B) The Birth of a Cultural Institution
(C) Opera Company Brought Opera to the Masses
(D) Controversy at New York City Opera
(E) Great American Composers

CONTINUE TO THE NEXT PAGE

27. In line 8 the term "poached" most nearly means

   (A) protected
   (B) coaxed away
   (C) rejected
   (D) infuriated
   (E) ignored

28. The author implies which of the following about the Metropolitan Opera?

   (A) It was more financially successful than the New York City Opera.
   (B) Its board prefers to stage operas by American composers.
   (C) It is well known for desegregating opera.
   (D) Its ticket prices are lower than most.
   (E) It has a limited season.

29. The tone of the entire passage can best be described as

   (A) mournful
   (B) critical
   (C) optimistic
   (D) indifferent
   (E) admiring

30. It can be inferred from the passage that American composers

   (A) often had performances at the Metropolitan Opera
   (B) choose to write in European languages
   (C) have trouble finding an audience
   (D) frequently compose music in forms other than operas
   (E) are better composers

CONTINUE TO THE NEXT PAGE

In the days of Babylonia's prosperity the Euphrates was hailed as "the soul of the land" and the Tigris as "the bestower of blessings". Skillful engineers had solved the problem of water distribution by irrigating sun-parched areas and preventing the excessive flooding of those districts which are now rendered

Line 5 impassable swamps when the rivers overflow. A network of canals was constructed throughout the country, which restricted the destructive tendencies of the Tigris and Euphrates and developed to a high degree their potentialities as fertilizing agencies.

The greatest of these canals appear to have been anciently river beds. One,
10 which is called Shatt en Nil to the north, and Shatt el Kar to the south, curved eastward from Babylon, and sweeping past Nippur, flowed like the letter S towards Larsa and then rejoined the river. It is believed to mark the course followed in the early Sumerian period by the Euphrates River, which has moved steadily westward many miles beyond the sites of ancient cities that were erected
15 on its banks.

Another important canal, the Shatt el Hai, crossed the plain from the Tigris to its sister river, which lies lower at this point, and does not run so fast. Where the artificial canals were constructed on higher levels than the streams which fed them, the water was raised by contrivances known as "shaddufs"; the
20 buckets or skin bags were roped to a weighted beam, with the aid of which they were swung up by workmen and emptied into the canals. It is possible that this toilsome mode of irrigation was substituted in favorable parts by the primitive water wheels, which are used in our own day by the inhabitants of the country who cultivate strips of land along the riverbanks.

31. It can be inferred from the passage that

(A) Babylonia had a series of effective leaders
(B) the success of Babylonia was due in large part to engineers
(C) the water wheel was never used in Babylonia
(D) in ancient times the Euphrates River lay west of where it currently runs
(E) canals were not important in Babylonia

CONTINUE TO THE NEXT PAGE

32. What was the purpose of the "weighted beam" (line 20)?

    (A) to move farm tools
    (B) to ensure the safety of workers
    (C) to limit water flow
    (D) to act as a foundation for a water wheel
    (E) to assist workers in raising water into canals

33. According to the passage, what were the two most important rivers in Babylonia?

    (A) Shatt en Nil and Shatt el Kar
    (B) Babylon and Nippur
    (C) Tigris and Euphrates
    (D) Shatt el Hai and Tigris
    (E) Shatt el Kar and Euphrates

34. Which of the following questions is answered by the passage?

    (A) How was water raised into the canals?
    (B) Who was the first leader of Babylonia?
    (C) What was the name of the engineer that invented the water wheel?
    (D) What led to the flooding of the rivers?
    (E) How often did the rivers flood?

35. The Tigris and Euphrates rivers are described as

    (A) minor
    (B) highly variable
    (C) unimportant to modern settlers of the river valley
    (D) in the same place that they were centuries ago
    (E) mainly forgotten

CONTINUE TO THE NEXT PAGE

Line 5

10

15

The next morning, Thursday, October 11th, it rained, as hard as ever; but we were determined to proceed on foot, nevertheless. We first made some inquiries with regard to the practicability of walking up the shore on the Atlantic side to Provincetown, whether we should meet with any creeks or marshes to trouble us. Higgins said that there was no obstruction, and that it was not much farther than by the road, but he thought that we should find it very "heavy" walking in the sand; it was bad enough in the road, a horse would sink in up to the fetlocks there. But there was one man at the tavern who had walked it, and he said that we could go very well, though it was sometimes inconvenient and even dangerous walking under the bank, when there was a great tide, with an easterly wind, which caused the sand to cave. For the first four or five miles we followed the road, which here turns to the north on the elbow, —the narrowest part of the Cape,—that we might clear an inlet from the ocean, a part of Nauset Harbor, in Orleans, on our right. We found the travelling good enough for walkers on the sides of the roads, though it was "heavy" for horses in the middle. We walked with our umbrellas behind us, since it blowed hard as well as rained, with driving mists, as the day before, and the wind helped us over the sand at a rapid rate. Everything indicated that we had reached a strange shore.

36. It can be inferred from the passage that the wind

   (A) was uncommon in Nauset Harbor
   (B) blew away the sand
   (C) determined the path that the narrator chose
   (D) made the narrator turn around
   (E) was blowing at the narrator's back

37. The phrase ""heavy" for horses" (line 15) refers to

   (A) horses being injured
   (B) horses only being able to carry light packages
   (C) the tendency of horses to avoid the rain
   (D) horses' hooves sinking into a muddy road
   (E) the natural tendency of horses to weigh a lot

CONTINUE TO THE NEXT PAGE

38. The passage implies

    (A) that the narrator has not been in a place like this before

    (B) it is safer to walk along the beach than to walk along the road

    (C) the narrator wishes he had stayed in the tavern

    (D) there are many creeks and marshes between the tavern and Provincetown

    (E) Higgins has never walked to Provincetown

39. The narrator can best be described as

    (A) lonely

    (B) reflective

    (C) determined

    (D) lazy

    (E) arrogant

40. In this passage, the author's primary purpose is to

    (A) provide directions to Provincetown

    (B) give a history of the Cape

    (C) explain how to care for horses

    (D) describe a treacherous journey on foot

    (E) discourage readers from visiting Provincetown

STOP

IF YOU HAVE TIME LEFT YOU MAY CHECK YOUR ANSWERS IN THIS SECTION ONLY

Section 3: Verbal

60 questions
30 minutes

This section has two types of questions- synonyms and analogies.

Synonyms

Directions: Each question has a word in all capital letters and then five answer choices that are in lower case letters. You need to choose the answer choice that has the word (or phrase) that is closest in meaning to the word that is in capital letters.

1. ADEQUATE:

   (A) sufficient
   (B) readily
   (C) explicit
   (D) favorable
   (E) sorrowful

2. CHAMPION:

   (A) disgrace
   (B) shift
   (C) welcome
   (D) support
   (E) deny

3. INTERFERE:

   (A) distribute
   (B) meddle
   (C) quantify
   (D) cherish
   (E) soothe

CONTINUE TO THE NEXT PAGE

4. DORMANT:

 (A) remote
 (B) enterprising
 (C) remarkable
 (D) ingenuous
 (E) inactive

5. OUTFIT:

 (A) move past
 (B) provide supplies
 (C) pick up
 (D) leave out
 (E) reveal

6. SEIZE:

 (A) fade
 (B) regret
 (C) take
 (D) fold
 (E) pounce

7. PORTION:

 (A) part
 (B) trough
 (C) food
 (D) scoop
 (E) density

8. INEPT:

 (A) boring
 (B) dizzy
 (C) successful
 (D) unskilled
 (E) decrepit

CONTINUE TO THE NEXT PAGE

9. GREENHORN:

   (A) committed fan
   (B) reluctant supporter
   (C) inexperienced person
   (D) strong opponent
   (E) recent retiree

10. DIMINUTIVE:

   (A) ominous
   (B) emerging
   (C) wretched
   (D) possible
   (E) tiny

11. SINGULAR:

   (A) careful
   (B) unique
   (C) deafening
   (D) crumbling
   (E) proposed

12. SECLUDED:

   (A) blossoming
   (B) overlooked
   (C) pronounced
   (D) private
   (E) tame

13. DELUGE:

   (A) downpour
   (B) traitor
   (C) package
   (D) squeak
   (E) comment

CONTINUE TO THE NEXT PAGE

14. LUMINOUS:

    (A) recent
    (B) shining
    (C) enormous
    (D) scratched
    (E) hanging

15. ODIOUS:

    (A) familiar
    (B) prosperous
    (C) disgusting
    (D) ideal
    (E) vindicated

16. REWARD:

    (A) lose
    (B) authorize
    (C) number
    (D) flinch
    (E) encourage

17. IRASCIBLE:

    (A) very hard
    (B) frequently late
    (C) easily annoyed
    (D) seldom consulted
    (E) without merit

18. PROSPECT:

    (A) fade
    (B) scowl
    (C) know
    (D) explore
    (E) scramble

CONTINUE TO THE NEXT PAGE

19. LAMPOON:

  (A) mock
  (B) light
  (C) abandon
  (D) possess
  (E) droop

20. GENTEEL:

  (A) envious
  (B) polite
  (C) practical
  (D) flickering
  (E) disturbed

21. AMBIGUOUS:

  (A) forgotten
  (B) maintained
  (C) level
  (D) unclear
  (E) peaceful

22. DEVIOUS:

  (A) weary
  (B) composed
  (C) playful
  (D) immediate
  (E) crafty

23. SPARSE:

  (A) fortified
  (B) wasteful
  (C) skimpy
  (D) gallant
  (E) coy

CONTINUE TO THE NEXT PAGE

24. DISLODGE:

  (A) certify
  (B) loosen
  (C) weigh
  (D) sacrifice
  (E) drift

25. ARDENT:

  (A) passionate
  (B) brief
  (C) profitable
  (D) effective
  (E) histrionic

26. PARTNER:

  (A) cushion
  (B) prune
  (C) accept
  (D) associate
  (E) indicate

27. REAP:

  (A) scurry
  (B) counsel
  (C) moisten
  (D) process
  (E) gather

28. TOLERABLE:

  (A) usable
  (B) dreadful
  (C) responsible
  (D) bearable
  (E) simple

CONTINUE TO THE NEXT PAGE

29. TABULATE:

- (A) encircle
- (B) repel
- (C) categorize
- (D) release
- (E) diffuse

30. COMPLACENT:

- (A) gleaming
- (B) smug
- (C) customary
- (D) inane
- (E) ferocious

CONTINUE TO THE NEXT PAGE

Analogies

Directions: Analogies questions ask you to identify the relationship between words. Choose the answer choice that best finishes the sentence.

31. Pallor is to color as

    (A) continuity is to shade
    (B) suspicion is to trust
    (C) praise is to support
    (D) dispatch is to speed
    (E) machination is to complaint

32. Spoon is to ladle as knife is to

    (A) fork
    (B) scissors
    (C) cleaver
    (D) drawer
    (E) rack

33. Hammer is to pounding as

    (A) screwdriver is to cutting
    (B) rain is to dampening
    (C) door is to entering
    (D) harness is to holding
    (E) bus is to driving

34. Conceited is to arrogant as industrious is to

    (A) lazy
    (B) glorified
    (C) condensed
    (D) dainty
    (E) hardworking

CONTINUE TO THE NEXT PAGE

35. Shell is to turtle as

   (A) armor is to knight
   (B) skin is to apple
   (C) hair is to human
   (D) thorax is to insect
   (E) can is to sugar

36. Bustle is to linger as

   (A) find is to locate
   (B) scoop is to make
   (C) soothe is to upset
   (D) reflect is to heal
   (E) rehearse is to practice

37. Reef is to fish as

   (A) husky is to dog
   (B) savannah is to lions
   (C) pellets is to hamster
   (D) rainforest is to zebras
   (E) horns is to bulls

38. Ask is to implore as

   (A) demand is to request
   (B) grease is to lubricate
   (C) retreat is to stumble
   (D) crank is to unwind
   (E) suggest is to declare

39. Caring is to trait as

   (A) miracle is to disaster
   (B) denial is to lawyer
   (C) minute is to hour
   (D) award is to praise
   (E) division is to contract

CONTINUE TO THE NEXT PAGE

40. Enigma is to perplexing as schemer is to

   (A) dishonest
   (B) successful
   (C) gracious
   (D) healthy
   (E) plump

41. Romantic is to sonnet as analytical is to

   (A) limerick
   (B) essay
   (C) haiku
   (D) advertisement
   (E) summary

42. Hook is to shepherd as torch is to

   (A) goat
   (B) herder
   (C) plumber
   (D) gardener
   (E) welder

43. Battery is to energy as

   (A) methane is to gas
   (B) degrees is to thermometer
   (C) tanker is to oil
   (D) license is to driver
   (E) oar is to swimmer

44. Valley is to chasm as

   (A) trench is to gorge
   (B) cliff is to mountain
   (C) flicker is to candle
   (D) gathering is to gala
   (E) melody is to harmony

CONTINUE TO THE NEXT PAGE

45. Rehearsal is to performance as

    (A) audition is to casting

    (B) musical is to comedy

    (C) chapter is to book

    (D) anthology is to stories

    (E) encore is to concert

46. Traitor is to secrets as

    (A) introduction is to conclusion

    (B) mystery is to thriller

    (C) seamstress is to needles

    (D) commander is to brigade

    (E) thief is to possessions

47. Clever is to ingenious as

    (A) persuasive is to argument

    (B) disgusting is to expensive

    (C) skilled is to expert

    (D) treacherous is to powerful

    (E) misguided is to decision

48. Movement is to ideals as

    (A) politics is to party

    (B) riot is to anger

    (C) college is to books

    (D) device is to tailor

    (E) strangers is to kindness

49. Tree is to bough as

    (A) leg is to torso

    (B) person is to arm

    (C) berry is to holly

    (D) evergreen is to pine

    (E) effect is to result

CONTINUE TO THE NEXT PAGE

50. Apprentice is to mentor as

   (A)   student is to professor
   (B)   graduate is to candidate
   (C)   boss is to employer
   (D)   principal is to leader
   (E)   electrician is to carpenter

51. Igloo is to ice as

   (A)   pipe is to house
   (B)   mansion is to hovel
   (C)   building is to car
   (D)   hut is to adobe
   (E)   steel is to skyscraper

52. Dull is to imagination as melancholy is to

   (A)   grudge
   (B)   discipline
   (C)   illusion
   (D)   definition
   (E)   joy

53. Hurt is to cripple as

   (A)   injure is to harm
   (B)   mean is to bully
   (C)   drizzle is to flood
   (D)   regard is to question
   (E)   observe is to record

54. Premonition is to forewarning as

   (A)   category is to difference
   (B)   scruple is to moral
   (C)   run is to sprint
   (D)   boredom is to amazement
   (E)   distort is to disprove

CONTINUE TO THE NEXT PAGE

55. Silent is to audible as

    (A)   tangible is to touchable

    (B)   heat is to visible

    (C)   cold is to scalding

    (D)   forced is to hilarious

    (E)   lengthy is to absent

56. Survey is to data as

    (A)   interview is to information

    (B)   poll is to winner

    (C)   graph is to line

    (D)   bandage is to heal

    (E)   quality is to quantity

57. Irritate is to antagonize as

    (A)   chop is to dice

    (B)   gulp is to sip

    (C)   fix is to mend

    (D)   embarrass is to mortify

    (E)   fret is to worry

58. Yawn is to sleepiness as

    (A)   stomp is to forgiveness

    (B)   clap is to hands

    (C)   growl is to bark

    (D)   linger is to delay

    (E)   sigh is to longing

59. Steadfast is to friend as

    (A)   fearless is to manager

    (B)   intellectual is to philosopher

    (C)   unique is to slogan

    (D)   deliberate is to meeting

    (E)   obedient is to cat

CONTINUE TO THE NEXT PAGE

60. Muffle is to sound as

    (A)   disturb is to sight

    (B)   remove is to ruin

    (C)   scrimp is to money

    (D)   hurdle is to obstacle

    (E)   freeze is to refrigerator

STOP

IF YOU HAVE TIME LEFT YOU MAY CHECK YOUR ANSWERS IN THIS SECTION ONLY

Section 4: Quantitative

25 questions

30 minutes

Directions: Each problem is followed by five answer choices. Figure out each problem and then decide which answer choice is best.

---

1. If $48 \div n = 48$, what is $48 - n$ equal to?

   (A) -1
   (B) 0
   (C) 1
   (D) 47
   (E) 48

---

2. $25 - 3\frac{1}{8} =$

   (A) $20\frac{7}{8}$

   (B) $21\frac{3}{8}$

   (C) $21\frac{7}{8}$

   (D) $22\frac{3}{8}$

   (E) $22\frac{7}{8}$

---

3. Which of the following is closest to the value of $8{,}058 \div 197$?

   (A) 6
   (B) 40
   (C) 50
   (D) 60
   (E) 400

CONTINUE TO THE NEXT PAGE

4. A machine can produce a metal blade in $\frac{3}{5}$ of a minute. What is the greatest number of metal blades that the machine can produce in one hour?

   (A) 100
   (B) 90
   (C) 72
   (D) 60
   (E) 36

5. $800.000 \times 0.0008 =$

   (A) 0.00064
   (B) 0.0064
   (C) 0.064
   (D) 0.64
   (E) 6.4

6. A music school has 75 violinists and 30 cellists. One third of the violinists also play piano, while one half of the cellists also play clarinet. How many more piano-playing violinists are there than clarinet-playing cellists?

   (A) 10
   (B) 20
   (C) 25
   (D) 35
   (E) 45

7. What is $2p^2 - 3q$ if $p = 4$ and $q = 9$?

   (A) -19
   (B) -11
   (C) 5
   (D) 27
   (E) 37

CONTINUE TO THE NEXT PAGE

8. $2\dfrac{4}{5} + 3\dfrac{3}{5} - 4\dfrac{4}{5} =$

    (A)   0.6
    (B)   1.3
    (C)   1.6
    (D)   2.3
    (E)   2.6

---

9. A pentagon has a perimeter of 35 inches. If each side of the pentagon is lengthened by 3 inches, what is the perimeter of the new pentagon?

    (A)   38 inches
    (B)   50 inches
    (C)   53 inches
    (D)   60 inches
    (E)   105 inches

---

10. 4 percent of what number is equal to 30?

    (A)   7.5
    (B)   120
    (C)   300
    (D)   750
    (E)   12,000

---

11. Arthur bought enough stone to cover a 30 by 60-foot patio for $2,700. How much did he pay per square foot for the stone?

    (A) $0.15
    (B) $0.45
    (C) $0.90
    (D) $1.05
    (E) $1.50

CONTINUE TO THE NEXT PAGE

12. $(-28) + 10 - (-20) =$

   (A) -38
   (B) -18
   (C) -8
   (D) 2
   (E) 22

---

13. In the xy-coordinate plane, the coordinates of point A are (5, 3) and the coordinates of point B are (–2, 4). What is the shortest distance from A to B?

   (A) $2\sqrt{2}$
   (B) $\sqrt{10}$
   (C) 5
   (D) $\sqrt{45}$
   (E) $5\sqrt{2}$

---

14. Which equation represents the statement, "Twenty-one is equal to six less than the product of three times one number and two times another number?"

   (A) $6 - 21 = 3n \times 2p$
   (B) $21 - 6 = 3n + 2p$
   (C) $21 = 3n - (2p + 6)$
   (D) $21 = (3n - 6) \times 2p$
   (E) $21 = (3n \times 2p) - 6$

---

15. Aaron ran the 8-lap race with an average time per lap of 1 minute and 13 seconds. How long did it take Aaron to complete the race?

   (A) 8 minutes and 24 seconds
   (B) 8 minutes and 54 seconds
   (C) 9 minutes and 5 seconds
   (D) 9 minutes and 44 seconds
   (E) 10 minutes and 8 seconds

CONTINUE TO THE NEXT PAGE

16. What percent of the following figure is shaded?

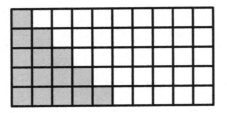

    (A)   15%
    (B)   25%
    (C)   30%
    (D)   45%
    (E)   70%

17. What is the value of the digit "3" in the number 765.432?

    (A)   3 thousandths
    (B)   3 hundredths
    (C)   3 tenths
    (D)   3 ones
    (E)   3 tens

18. Which is equivalent to $(x^2 + 3x - 5)(x^2 - 3x + 7)$?

    (A) $x^4 - 9x^2 - 35$
    (B) $x^4 - 6x^3 - 7x^2 - 36x - 35$
    (C) $x^4 + 6x^3 - 7x^2 - 36x - 35$
    (D) $x^4 - 7x^2 + 36x - 35$
    (E) $x^4 - 7x^2 - 36x - 35$

CONTINUE TO THE NEXT PAGE

19. Austin has a coin jar with p pennies, 4 nickels, d dimes, and q quarters. Which expression will give Austin the value of his coins in cents?

(A) $25q + 10d + p + 20$
(B) $q + 5d + 25p + 20$
(C) $(p + d + q) \times (1 + 4 + 10 + 25)$
(D) $q \div 25 + d \div 10 + p + 4$
(E) $q \div 4 + d \div 10 + p \div 100 + 20$

---

20. $3083 \div 8 =$

(A) $\dfrac{3000}{8} + \dfrac{800}{8} + \dfrac{3}{8}$

(B) $\dfrac{3000}{8} \times \dfrac{83}{8}$

(C) $\dfrac{3000}{8} + \dfrac{80}{8} + \dfrac{3}{8}$

(D) $\dfrac{30}{8} \times \dfrac{8}{8} \times \dfrac{3}{8}$

(E) $\dfrac{3000}{8000} + \dfrac{80}{80} + \dfrac{3}{8}$

---

21. Which of the following is a multiple of 13, given that $x + y$ is a multiple of 13?

(A) $x \div 13 + y \div 13$
(B) $x + 13 + y$
(C) $x \times (13 - y) + y \times (13 - x)$
(D) $(x - 13)^2 + (y - 13)^2$
(E) $y + 13 - x$

---

22. Points A, B, and C are the vertices of a triangle. The length of side AB is t. Side BC is twice as long as side AB. The length of side AC is 5 less than the length of side BC. What is the perimeter of triangle ABC?

(A) $3t - 5$
(B) $3t + 5$
(C) $4t - 5$
(D) $4t + 5$
(E) $5t - 5$

CONTINUE TO THE NEXT PAGE

23. 500 families who own at least one truck or van were polled about their vehicles. If 350 own a truck and 300 own a van, then how many families own both a truck and a van?

    (A) 50
    (B) 100
    (C) 150
    (D) 500
    (E) 650

24. For a positive even number, p, which of the following expressions has the greatest value?

    (A) $p^2 - p$

    (B) $p - 1$

    (C) $1 - p$

    (D) $\dfrac{1}{p - 1}$

    (E) $\dfrac{1}{p + 1}$

25. If $2x = 3y$ and $4y = 5z$, what is the value of $\dfrac{x}{z}$?

    (A) $\dfrac{8}{15}$

    (B) $\dfrac{15}{8}$

    (C) 3

    (D) 7

    (E) 8

STOP

IF YOU HAVE TIME LEFT YOU MAY CHECK YOUR ANSWERS IN THIS SECTION ONLY

Answers

Answers to Section 1: Quantitative

Correct Answers	Your Answers	Answered Correctly	Answered Incorrectly	Omitted
1. D				
2. B				
3. A				
4. E				
5. B				
6. C				
7. C				
8. E				
9. D				
10. E				
11. A				
12. E				
13. A				
14. B				
15. D				
16. E				
17. E				
18. D				
19. D				
20. B				
21. A				
22. C				
23. D				
24. B				
25. D				
Total				

Raw score = Total # answered correctly _____ − total # answered incorrectly _____ ÷ 4

Your raw score: _____

Answers to Section 2: Reading Comprehension

Correct Answers	Your Answers	Answered Correctly	Answered Incorrectly	Omitted
1. C				
2. A				
3. E				
4. B				
5. D				
6. D				
7. A				
8. C				
9. E				
10. B				
11. A				
12. D				
13. C				
14. B				
15. E				
16. C				
17. A				
18. D				
19. B				
20. E				
21. A				
22. B				
23. E				
24. C				
25. D				
26. C				
27. B				
28. A				
29. E				
30. D				
31. B				
32. E				

33. C				
34. A				
35. B				
36. E				
37. D				
38. A				
39. C				
40. D				
Total				

Raw score = Total # answered correctly _____ – total # answered incorrectly _____ ÷ 4

Your raw score: _____

Answers to Section 3: Verbal

Correct Answer	Your Answer	Answered Correctly	Answered Incorrectly	Omitted
1. A				
2. D				
3. B				
4. E				
5. B				
6. C				
7. A				
8. D				
9. C				
10. E				
11. B				
12. D				
13. A				
14. B				
15. C				
16. E				
17. C				
18. D				
19. A				
20. B				
21. D				
22. E				
23. C				
24. B				
25. A				
26. D				
27. E				
28. D				
29. C				
30. B				
31. B				
32. C				

33. D				
34. E				
35. A				
36. C				
37. B				
38. E				
39. D				
40. A				
41. B				
42. E				
43. C				
44. D				
45. A				
46. E				
47. C				
48. B				
49. B				
50. A				
51. D				
52. E				
53. C				
54. B				
55. C				
56. A				
57. D				
58. E				
59. B				
60. C				
Total				

Raw score = Total # answered correctly _____ – total # answered incorrectly _____ ÷ 4

Your raw score: _____

Answers to Section 4: Quantitative

Correct Answers	Your Answers	Answered Correctly	Answered Incorrectly	Omitted
1. D				
2. C				
3. B				
4. A				
5. D				
6. A				
7. C				
8. C				
9. B				
10. D				
11. E				
12. D				
13. E				
14. E				
15. D				
16. C				
17. B				
18. D				
19. A				
20. C				
21. B				
22. E				
23. C				
24. A				
25. B				
Total				

Raw score = Total # answered correctly _____ – total # answered incorrectly _____ ÷ 4

Your raw score: _____

Interpreting your scores

On the SSAT, your raw score is the number of questions that you answered correctly on each section minus the number of questions you answered incorrectly divided by 4. Nothing is added or subtracted for the questions that you omit.

Your raw score is then converted into a scaled score. This scaled score is then converted into a percentile score. Remember that it is the percentile score that schools are looking at. Your percentile score compares you only to other students in your grade.

Below is a chart that gives a very rough conversion between your raw score on the practice test and a percentile score.

PLEASE NOTE – The purpose of this chart is to let you see how the scoring works, not to give you an accurate percentile score. You will need to complete the practice test in *The Official Guide to the Upper Level SSAT* in order to get a more accurate percentile score.

Approximate raw score needed for 50th percentile		
Section 1 + Section 4: Quantitative	Section 2: Reading comprehension	Section 3: Verbal
28-32	20-24	24-28

Looking for more instruction and practice?

Check out these other titles for the Upper Level SSAT:

Success on the Upper Level SSAT: A Complete Course

- ✓ Strategies to use for each section of the Upper Level SSAT
- ✓ Reading and vocabulary drills
- ✓ In-depth math content instruction with practice sets
- ✓ 1 full-length practice test (different from the practice tests in *The Best Unofficial Practice Tests for the Upper Level SSAT*)

30 Days to Acing the Upper Level SSAT

- ✓ 15 "workouts" – each a 30-minute exercise with vocabulary and practice questions for every multiple-choice section of the test
- ✓ Test-taking strategies for each section

Books by Test Prep Works

	Content instruction	Test-taking strategies	Practice problems	Full-length practice tests
ISEE				
Lower Level (for students applying for admission to grades 5-6)				
Success on the Lower Level ISEE	✓	✓	✓	✓ (1)
30 Days to Acing the Lower Level ISEE		✓	✓	
The Best Unofficial Practice Tests for the Lower Level ISEE				✓ (2)
Middle Level (for students applying for admission to grades 7-8)				
Success on the Middle Level ISEE	✓	✓	✓	✓ (1)
The Best Unofficial Practice Tests for the Middle Level ISEE				✓ (2)
Upper Level (for students applying for admission to grades 9-12)				
Success on the Upper Level ISEE	✓	✓	✓	✓ (1)
The Best Unofficial Practice Tests for the Upper Level ISEE				✓ (2)
SSAT				
Middle Level (for students applying for admission to grades 6-8)				
Success on the Middle Level SSAT	✓	✓	✓	✓ (1)
The Best Unofficial Practice Tests for the Middle Level SSAT				✓ (2)
Upper Level (for students applying for admission to grades 9-12)				
Success on the Upper Level SSAT	✓	✓	✓	✓ (1)
30 Days to Acing the Upper Level SSAT		✓	✓	
The Best Unofficial Practice Tests for the Upper Level SSAT				✓ (2)

TEST PREP WORKS, LLC.

Made in the USA
Middletown, DE
23 September 2019